THE BEST
ESL CONVERSATION QUESTIONS

100 At-A-Glance Lesson Plans for the ESL Classroom

BY

Fran O'Brien

The Best ESL Conversation Questions
100 At-A-Glance Lesson Plans for the ESL Classroom
Copyright © 2015 Fran O'Brien
All rights reserved.
ISBN-13: 978-1502410092
ISBN-10: 1502410095

Available on Amazon.com and other online bookstores.

Further information and resources at:
www.eslconversationquestionsonline.com

Table of Contents

ACKNOWLEDGEMENTS 8

INTRODUCTION 9

    Extra Resources and Website 9

    Who Is This Book For? 9

    Why Use Questions? 9

12 STEP QUICK-START GUIDE TO TEACHING CONVERSATION 10

    Step 1: Set Lesson Goals 10

    Step 2: Warm Up 10

    Step 3: Don't Allow Polar Answers 10

    Step 4: Maximise Student Talk-Time 10

    Step 5: Vocabulary and Grammar 11

    Step 6: Correct Students 11

    Step 7: Provide Variety 12

    Step 8: Give Instructions and Timeframes 12

    Step 9: Take Notes During Communication Activities 13

    Step 10: Correct Students after Pair or Group Work 13

    Step 11: Be a Facilitator (Not a Participant) 13

    Step 12: Give Feedback 14

CONVERSATION TOPICS 15

    Advice 16

    Airlines and Flying 17

    Alternative Energy 18

    Alternative Medicine 20

    Ambition 21

    Appearance 22

    Body language 23

    Books and Reading 24

Career Paths	25
Cars and Driving	26
Change and Transitions	27
Childhood	28
Cities	29
Communication	30
Commuting	31
Cooking	33
Cultural Differences	34
Customer Service	35
CVs/Résumés	36
Decisions	37
Emergencies and Accidents	38
Employment	40
Entrepreneurs	42
Environment	43
Ethical Eating	44
Family Life	46
Fashion	47
Festivals and Celebrations	48
First Impressions	49
Food	50
Friends	51
Future Predictions	52
Gaming	54
Gender Roles	55
Gender Roles in the Workplace	56
Globalisation	57
Habits	58
Having Children	59

- Health 60
- Healthy Living and Exercise 61
- Healthy Eating 62
- Heroes and Heroines 63
- History 64
- Hobbies 65
- Holidays/Vacations 66
- Homes and Houses 67
- Hometowns 68
- Honesty and Lying 69
- Hotels 70
- Individuality 72
- Innovation and Creativity 73
- Intelligence 74
- Internet 75
- Investing 76
- Job Interviews 77
- Jobs 78
- Job Search 79
- Leadership Styles 80
- Marketing 81
- Meetings 82
- Memory 83
- Money 84
- Motivation 85
- Movies 86
- Networking 87
- News and Media 88
- Nuclear Power 89
- Occasions 90

- Parenting 91
- Performance Reviews and Feedback 92
- Personality 93
- Privacy and Data Protection 94
- Productivity 95
- Qualifications 96
- Relationships 97
- Remedies 98
- Responsibility 99
- Restaurants 100
- Routines 101
- Sales 102
- School and Education 103
- Senses 104
- Shopping 105
- Small Talk 106
- Smoking 107
- Social Networking 108
- Sports 109
- Stress 110
- Success 111
- Superstitions 112
- Technology 113
- Television 114
- Time 115
- Traditions & Customs 116
- Transport 117
- Travel 118
- Vegetarian and Vegan 119
- Weddings 120

Work-Life Balance 121
Youth and Aging 122

Acknowledgements

My heartfelt thanks to my partner Regina for supporting and putting up with me during yet another project and to my beautiful daughter Clara for making me feel like the luckiest person on Earth every time I lay eyes on her!

A huge thank-you to my sister Martha for her encouragement, suggestions and shoulder to cry on!

Last but not least, I want to thank my parents Mary Claire and Chris for their love, support and humour throughout the years.

Introduction

Extra Resources and Website

Thank you for purchasing this book and congratulations on finding a teaching resource that will help you give structured, effective lessons as well as save you many hours of preparation.

For more free lesson plans and resources check out the website that accompanies this book at www.eslconversationquestionsonline.com.

Who Is This Book For?

This book is for ESL teachers that want to encourage their pupils to practice the target language in a natural setting, i.e. in conversation. Pupils will need a reasonable level of spoken English to use this material. Generally speaking, the lesson plans in this book can be used with pupils of lower-intermediate level (or better), though a handful of topics require a slightly better grasp of the language.

Pupils at the lower end of this spectrum may need a little more practice of the key vocabulary and structures associated with a topic so that they are better 'primed' to discuss the topic in question.

Why Use Questions?

Questions are the mainstay of the ESL conversation lesson. Questions inspire thoughts, opinions and reactions, all of which can be used to practice the language in a natural way. Since our natural inclination upon hearing a question is to answer it, questions present one of the easiest ways to keep your students talking.

I hope that you enjoy using this book and that you find this resource useful.

12 Step Quick-Start Guide to Teaching Conversation

Step 1: Set Lesson Goals

It is beneficial for students to know what the objective of the lesson is and why the objective is important. For this reason, it is helpful to write a clear lesson goal on the board at the beginning of the lesson.

For example:

- Learning Objective: To be able to discuss the advantages and disadvantages of alternative energies.
- Learning objective: To learn and practice vocabulary related to the topic 'Technology' and to be able to discuss how technology changes our lives.

Step 2: Warm Up

The purpose of a 'warm-up' is to get students thinking about a topic and their associations, feelings, opinions and attitudes towards that topic.

This can take many forms:

- Some 'easy' introductory questions from the teacher (I've provided these for each topic)
- Brainstorming vocabulary pupils already know related to the topic
- Showing a picture related to the topic and getting pupils to describe it
- Pupils sharing their first associations with a topic
- Asking students to react to realia
- Anything else that 'sets the scene...'

Pupils often need a little thinking time to 'get into' a topic, so it's generally better not to bombard them with difficult questions at the beginning, as some pupils can feel 'put on the spot.'

Step 3: Don't Allow Polar Answers

Don't allow your students to answer "Yes" or "No" and leave it at that! It will probably be a short discussion! Always ask "Why?" or insist they elaborate. Anything else is simply a waste of good questions!

Step 4: Maximise Student Talk-Time

How much time do you spend talking in your lessons and how much do your pupils spend talking? It is often useful to reflect on this and even to try and put a percentage on it.

Generally speaking, 'teacher talk-time' should be highest in initial phase of the lesson when warming up, introducing and practicing new vocabulary, etc., after which pupils should have *an increasingly independent role*.

Step 5: Vocabulary and Grammar

The focus of a conversation lesson is generally fluency, not accuracy. However, students may need a grammar structure to complete a task, or (more likely) vocabulary to discuss a topic.

Vocabulary is necessary. I like to circle the topic on the board and write vocabulary as a mind-map around it as I introduce each word. Vocabulary gets students thinking about the topic, so it also serves a purpose by setting the scene. If left on the board, the mind map can be re-used in the feedback phase at the very end of the lesson (see point 12 below).

If grammar structures are necessary, keep it short and limit it to the structure necessary to complete the tasks ahead.

Step 6: Correct Students

As mentioned above, the focus of a conversation lesson is fluency rather than accuracy. However, this does not mean that it is bad to correct students! Obviously, you don't want to correct so much that it damages and interrupts the 'flow' of the conversation. However, during the phases of the lesson in which you are interacting directly with a student (e.g. asking them a question, listening to them report pair work results to you etc.), corrections are fine!

Corrections can come from 3 sources:
- From the pupil themselves (self-correction)
- From classmates (peer correction)
- From the teacher

In fact, this is the order corrections should take! Always try to get students to correct themselves first. If that doesn't bear fruit, ask for peer correction. Failing that, correct the pupil yourself.

Let's say a student makes the following mistake: "I have lived in this city since 10 years."

Step 1: Use a facial expression (catch the student's eye and raise your eyebrows, for example) to let the student know that you have noticed a mistake and to invite them to correct it.

If the student cannot self correct...

Step 2: *Bring* the student to the mistake, by saying "I have lived in this city...?", and wait for the student to complete the sentence. This tells the student *where* the mistake is in the sentence.

If the student *still* cannot self correct...

Step 3: Ask for a peer-correction: "Anyone?", or "Can anyone help Sandra out?"

If nobody can correct the mistake...

Step 4: Ask a question that contains a hint: "Have you lived in this city *for* 10 years?"

Failing that, simply give the correct sentence. *Always* insist the student repeats the correct sentence *in full*.

Step 7: Provide Variety

There is simply nothing worse than having a group of bored ESL students in front of you. For this reason, one of the most important roles of the ESL teacher is to **provide variety**.

This can be done (a) on a content level, by providing a variety of contrasting tasks and (b) on a 'people' level, i.e. students work with different partners, in pairs, small groups, larger groups, circulate and talk to a number of different people etc.

Students experience this as variety.

This book has been designed to provide you with variety on both of these levels, but let's take a quick look at the different pupil combinations that are possible:

- Teacher asks pupil
- Pupil asks teacher
- One pupil selects and asks other pupils from the class
- Pupil asks pupil (pair work)
- One pair gets together with another pair to compare their results from an activity
- 3 pupils ask each other and discuss
- Pupils stand up, circulate and ask different people (i.e. cocktail-party style)

It is often helpful to plan a lesson in terms of a succession of short phases (anything between 5 and 20 minutes), with each phase having a different task and pupil combination.

Unless you have a very small class, you should try to avoid pupils working with the same partner twice.

Step 8: Give Instructions and Time Frames

Before allowing pupils to work independently (communication activities, speaking activities, partner interviews, consolidation activities etc.) it is important to give (a) clear instructions and (b) a clear time frame for the task.

To make sure pupils have understood, it can be helpful to have pupils 'echo' it back to you:

"Sandra, what do you have to do?" "David, how much time do you have?"

Also, try to give pupils a warning a few minutes before the independent phase of the activity ends: "Okay, 2 minutes left!"

Step 9: Take Notes During Communication Activities

Communication activities encompass any activity that gives pupils the chance to use the language independently. In this book they are referred to as 'Speaking Activities', 'Partner Interviews' or 'Consolidations Activities.' These activities vary in nature and objective: planning, narrating, prioritizing, justifying, comparing, listing, deciding, problem solving, summarizing and role playing.

While students are involved in a communication activity, take note of any issues for correction that you hear on a piece of paper. Also listen out for things students are doing *well*. It can be helpful to divide a page in half with positives on one half and points for improvement on the other.

These points can be used to give feedback either directly after the communication activity or at the end of the lesson to give feedback and praise.

Step 10: Correct Students after Pair or Group Work

After speaking activities, partner interviews and consolidation activities (independent work) it is important to have students report their results to you (and to the class).

This gives you the opportunity to correct their English (see correction strategies above), provides all-important variety and, if you wish, can lead to a fruitful class discussion in which the different results are compared.

When doing this with partner interviews (or any other task in which a student needs to find out information from another student) it is very useful to have students report what their *partner* said: "Sandra, what did David tell you?" and then: "David, what did Sandra tell you?"

The reason for this is as follows: If you only ever ask a pupil about their *own* opinions, pupils get used to using the 1st person form of the verb. By reporting what their partner said the pupil is forced to use (and practice) the 3rd person form.

By the way, a good way of correcting a student who forgets the 'S' on the he/she/it form of the verb is to trace an 'S-shape' in the air with your finger. Just make sure to trace it backwards, so that it appears the right way around to the pupil!

Step 11: Be a Facilitator (Not a Participant)

While it may be tempting to contribute your own opinions to a discussion (especially when a discussion becomes interesting) this is, generally speaking, a waste of students' talk-time.

A conversation lesson should be the pupils' space to express themselves, so try to see yourself as a facilitator rather than a participant in the discussion.

Step 12: Give Feedback

Set aside 5-10 minutes at the end of each lesson for giving feedback.

The feedback section of a lesson serves two purposes:
- It tells you if the student has understood what you were trying to teach them.
- It makes the student aware of how much he/she has learned.

For example, if learning vocabulary related to a particular topic is the goal of the lesson, and it is still written on the board, you could ask individual students to create a sentence with that piece of vocabulary or ask a student a question that forces them to use the piece of vocabulary in the reply.

This demonstrates *to you* that the student can use the new vocabulary and *to the student* that they have learnt something. It's nice to tick the vocabulary off as soon as it has been used correctly.

At the end of a lesson it is good practice to return to the goal and ask students if they feel they have achieved it, and then tick it off.

CONVERSATION TOPICS

Advice

Warm-up

Are you good at giving advice? Do many people come to you with their problems? If you could go back in time and give your younger self some advice, what would it be?

Key Vocabulary

advice (n.) / advise (v.) / to suggest / to recommend / you should... / to regret

Teacher → Pupil Questions

- Who do you go to when you need advice? Why?
- What advice will you give your children?
- Have you ever visited a careers advisor? Did you find their advice helpful?
- Do you have any regrets about the decisions you have made in life? What advice do you wish you had been given?
- Did your parents give you good advice when you were younger? What was it?

Speaking activity

Write down one problem you have on which you would like to be given some advice.

If you could ask anyone in the world for advice, whom would you ask? What do you think they would say? Take a few moments to write down your thoughts.

Report to the class.

Partner Interview

- What advice would you give the leader of your country?
- What is the best/worst piece of advice you have ever been given?
- Are you the kind of person who listens to other peoples' advice? Why/why not?
- Has anyone ever given you the wrong advice? What happened?
- Have *you* ever given the wrong advice? Tell the story.

Consolidation

Stand up, circulate and ask each of your classmates for advice on the problem you wrote down earlier. Get advice from everyone.

Who gave the best advice? Why? Report to the class.

Airlines and Flying

Warm-up

Do you enjoy flying? What do you like/dislike about it? What is your favourite airline? Why?

Key Vocabulary

to prefer / I rather... than... / smooth / bumpy / turbulence / nervous / afraid of / more space / to queue / baggage / hand luggage / carry-on bag / takeoff (n.) / to take off (v.) / landing

Teacher → Pupil Questions

- Do you prefer budget or luxury airlines? Why?
- What was your worst flying experience? What was the problem? Was it a bumpy flight? Was there a problem with the booking?
- What was your best flying experience? What made it so good?
- Are you nervous flyer? If so, why? Have you had a bad flying experience?

Speaking activity

What is most important to you when choosing a flight: (a) service, (b) price, (c) comfort, (d) flexibility, (e) baggage allowance, (f) leg room? Re-write the list in order of importance.

Then show your list to a classmate and explain *why* you find these things important.

Partner Interview

- Do you prefer to travel by air or over land, e.g. by train? What are the pros and cons?
- Compare two airlines you have travelled with in the past. Which was better and why?
- Compare economy, business class and first class. What are the biggest differences?
- "I don't mind flying, but I hate getting to the airport, queuing, checking in bags, going through security and all the things that go along with it!" Do these things annoy you, too?

Consolidation: Role Play

Role A: You work for Transnational Airways. Your airline has a policy of overbooking flights (usually one customer doesn't show up). You are about to fly from San Francisco to New York. First class is overbooked, but you have a free seat in economy class. Tell the next customer there is no first class seat and offer them the seat in economy class. Offer a concession to the passenger to make it up to them. A customer is approaching you now.

Role B: You have had a long week travelling on business and you are about to fly from San Francisco to New York. You are very tired. You have booked an expensive first class seat so that you can lie flat and sleep on the flight. Greet the airline employee at the check-in desk.

Alternative Energy

Warm-up

Would you be willing to pay more for electricity if it came from renewable energy sources? Do you know how the energy you use in your home is produced? Do you try to save energy in your home? In what ways?

Key Vocabulary

renewable / non-renewable / source / resource / fossil fuel / geothermal / solar / biomass / tidal / carbon-dioxide / greenhouse effect / global warming / to generate (electricity)

Teacher → Pupil Questions

- Do you think there will be a major war over finite fossil fuels in the next 100 years?
- How dependent is your country on non-renewable energy sources?
- Has your country taken any steps to reduce its dependence on non-renewable energy sources?
- Which source of renewable energy do you think will be used most in your country in the future?
- Would you invest in 'green' investments? Why/why not?

Speaking activity

Tell a partner everything you know about the following forms of alternative energy:
- Solar energy
- Wind energy
- Tidal energy
- Biomass energy
- Geothermal energy

Pool your knowledge with the rest of the group to try to learn more and get a more complete picture.

Partner Interview

- Would you consider powering your home using solar panels? What are the pros and cons of doing so?
- Which form of alternative energy 'ticks the most boxes', in your opinion? Which will be used most in the future?
- Do you think all countries will ever sign the Kyoto protocol? Why/why not?
- Do you think governments do enough to address environmental issues?
- Do you think alternative energies should be subsidised by governments? What are the pros and cons of doing this?

Consolidation

You are on the board of directors of a large chemical corporation. Your company uses a huge amount of energy to produce its products. You get most of this energy from non-renewable energy sources. Recently, however, your government has passed a law stating that all companies of your size must get 80% of their energy from renewable sources. Your company has decided to invest in the infrastructure to achieve this. However, you still need the most cost-effective solution to fulfil your considerable energy needs.

Your company is located 400 kilometres from the coast in a northern European country. There is a small river nearby.

Discuss the pros and cons of the different options with the other directors on the board and come to an agreement about which would be best for your company.

Alternative Medicine

Warm-up

Do you think you need to believe in alternative medicines for them to work? Which alternative medicines do you trust? Which do you not trust? If you had a serious illness, would you go to an alternative medicine practitioner?

Key Vocabulary

to believe in something / the placebo effect / to get ill / to get better / health insurance

Teacher → Pupil Questions

- Do you think of non-western medicine as 'alternative' medicine (e.g. traditional Chinese medicine)?
- Do you ever worry about the side effects of prescription drugs?
- Have you ever/would you ever try acupuncture? Does the therapy appeal to you? Why/why not?
- If a medicine makes a patient feel better through the placebo effect, isn't that just as good as a 'proven' medicine?

Speaking activity

Stand up, circulate and ask your classmates if they have ever tried alternative medicine. Was the experience positive, negative or neutral?

What is the prevailing attitude towards alternative medicine in the class? Report.

Partner Interview

- Do you think alternative medicines and practitioners should be regulated like standard medicine?
- Do you think it makes any difference if a medicine is 'natural' or is created in a laboratory? Does the word 'natural' have a feel-good factor associated with it?
- 'Food is the best medicine.' Do you agree or disagree?
- In Norway, the government has begun integrating alternative medicine into the national health insurance system. Do you think alternative therapies should be paid for by health insurance, even if it makes the insurance more expensive?

Consolidation

What advantages does alternative medicine have over standard medicine? What advantages does standard medicine have over alternative medicine?

Discuss with a partner and present your ideas to the class.

Ambition

Warm-up

Are you the kind of person who tries hard to achieve goals? Is it a good thing to be ambitious, in your opinion? Were you ambitious when you were younger? Did you want to succeed in school?

Key Vocabulary

to persevere / to try hard / to strive / to achieve / to succeed / career / obituary / goals / aims / targets / promotion / to get promoted / status / motivated / eager / driven

Teacher → Pupil Questions

- Do you think ambitious people are happier than unambitious people, or vice versa?
- Do you prefer ambitious people or unambitious people?
- Are you ambitious in terms of your career? What about in your private life and in sports?
- Do you think you will get more ambitious or less ambitious as you get older?

Speaking activity

Discuss with a partner: Which gender do you think are more ambitious, women or men? Are men and women ambitious in different ways? If so, why do these differences exist? Nature? Nurture? Expectations? Testosterone levels?

Make a short list of the differences you have noticed between men and women when it comes to ambition. Then share your list with the class.

Partner Interview

- Who is the most ambitious person you know? How does their ambition express itself?
- Have you ever had an ambition that you failed to realise? What effect did this have on you? Did you give up or try harder?
- Are the people in your family very ambitious?
- Do you think it is a good idea to encourage children to be ambitious, or do you think this puts children under too much pressure?
- What would you like your own obituary to say? What achievements would you like included?

Consolidation

Ask a partner what they would like to have achieved (a) in 5 years, (b) in 10 years and (c) in 20 years.

Then report to the class if you think your partner's ambitions and goals are realistic and how ambitious you think your partner is. Give reasons for your answer.

Appearance

Warm-up

Do you think beauty helps you to be successful? In which jobs is beauty linked to success?

Key Vocabulary

body image / attractive / to be under pressure / eating disorder / diet / slender / large / fit / beauty products / plastic surgery / height / short / tall / ugly / muscular

Teacher → Pupil Questions

- Do you think people from other cultures see beauty differently?
- Do you think people spend too much time and money on beauty?
- How will you think about beauty at the age of 80?
- Do you think the media portray an unrealistic image of beauty?

Speaking activity

www.darwinsdating.com is a dating website for beautiful people only. When you submit a profile, other members vote if you are beautiful enough for your profile to appear on the site.

Ask a partner about their opinion of this idea.

Partner Interview

- Would you prefer to be intelligent or beautiful?
- Would you prefer to be wealthy or beautiful?
- What is your opinion of beauty contests?
- 'The media decides what is beautiful or ugly.' Do you agree or disagree?
- 'Our so-called 'ideal' body image puts people (especially young people) under huge pressure and doesn't acknowledge that people come in all shapes and sizes.' What is your opinion?

Consolidation

In the 19th century pale, white skin was considered beautiful. With a partner, discuss what you think will be considered beautiful in 100 years. Consider skin colour, body image, hairstyle and clothing.

Share your ideas with the class.

Body language

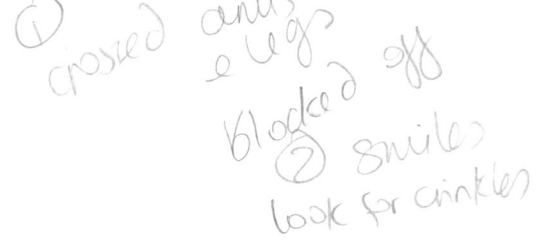

Warm-up

When you meet someone new, which body language do you notice first (posture, gestures, etc.)? How much attention do you pay to other people's body language? How much attention do you pay to your own?

Key Vocabulary

posture / gestures / to interpret / reliable / eye-contact / male / female / appropriate / victorious / depressed / bored / interested / confident

Teacher → Pupil Questions

- ☐ Are you good at interpreting body language?
- ☐ Do you think body language is a reliable source of information?
- ☐ Have you ever interpreted someone's body language incorrectly? What happened?
- ☐ What kind of handshake do you like? What kind do you dislike?
- ☐ How do *you* shake hands? What do you think someone's handshake says about them?

Speaking activity

Discuss with a partner: How is men's body language different from women's body language?

Come up with 3 situations and contrast typical male and female body language in each situation.

Report to the class.

Partner Interview

- ☐ What is the first thing someone would notice about body language in your culture?
- ☐ How close do you like someone to stand when you are having a conversation? How close is too close? Have you noticed if this is different in other cultures?
- ☐ Do you use a lot of gestures in your culture? Do you like it when someone uses gestures?
- ☐ What kind of eye contact is appropriate when you are (a) talking and (b) listening?

Consolidation

Discuss with a partner: Describe what body language someone uses when they are feeling:

- Victorious
- Depressed
- Bored
- Interested
- Confident

Books and Reading

Warm-up

Do you read mainly for information or for entertainment? Who is your favourite author? Which newspapers/magazines do you read and why? What is your favourite genre? Do you prefer fiction or non-fiction?

Key Vocabulary

author / genre / plot / character / fiction / non-fiction / reviews / to judge a book by its cover

Teacher → Pupil Questions

- Do you read books based on recommendations? Where do you go to get book recommendations or reviews?
- Have your reading habits changed since you were a child/teenager? How?
- Have you ever read a book more than once? If so, why?
- Did you enjoy reading books in school?

Speaking activity

Discuss with a partner: Do you prefer or eBooks or printed books? Do you think printed books will die out eventually? What role will printed books play in the future?

With a partner, list the advantages and disadvantages of eBooks versus printed books.

Share your ideas with the class.

Partner Interview

- What books would you recommend to other people?
- What factors are important to you when choosing a book to read? Author? Cover design? Genre?
- 'You can't judge a book by its cover.' Industry experts say this is *exactly* what people do, however! How important is the cover of a book, in your opinion?
- Have you ever watched a film based on a book you had read? Which was better and why?

Consolidation

Choose a book you found especially interesting and give a partner a 'verbal review' of the book. Include:

- An outline of the plot
- A description of the main characters
- Information about the author and writing style
- A few positives and negatives

Career Paths

Warm-up

Can you describe your career path so far? What are your future career plans? Are you happy with how your career is progressing?

Key Vocabulary

interested in / responsible for / ambitious / field / to decide on / profession / promotion / opportunities / salary / professional growth

Teacher → Pupil Questions

- How did you decide on your current profession?
- How did you get interested in that area? Were you interested in similar things as a child?
- Did you choose a job compatible with your interests?
- Did you end up in your profession by chance or by choice?
- Are you ambitious in terms of your career?

Speaking activity - Role Play

Role A: You are a professional careers advisor and you are about to see a new client. Ask them about their career goals and advise them how they can reach their goals.

Role B: You wish to move up the corporate ladder. You have decided to consult a careers advisor. Tell the careers advisor about your career so far and your goals for the future. Ask for advice.

Partner Interview

- Do you get the chance to use your talents in your job?
- Have you ever changed careers? Why? What was your motivation?
- What are the fastest growing professions in your country?
- If you had to change jobs what field would you go into?
- Which professions will still exist in 50 years? Which will not exist?

Consolidation

When considering a company to work for, how important to you are (a) opportunities for promotion, (b) colleagues, (c) atmosphere, (d) management, (e) salary, (f) professional growth?

Put the list above in order of priority, starting with the most important factor for you.

Share your list with the class and explain your choices.

Cars and Driving

Warm-up

If you could buy any car in the world, which car would you choose? Do you think of your car as a status symbol, or just as something that gets you from A to B?

Key Vocabulary

car dealer / environment / to negotiate / status symbol / luxury / budget model

Teacher → Pupil Questions

- Do you buy new or second-hand cars? What are the advantages and disadvantages?
- Do you consider the environment when buying a car? Would you ever consider buying a hybrid or electric car?
- How do you think cars will change in the next 50 years?
- Which car brands would you recommend to a friend? Why?
- Which car brands don't you recommend? Why don't you recommend them?

Speaking activity

You are thinking of buying a new car. Stand up, circulate and ask each classmate for a review of the car they drive.

Tell the class which review convinced you and why.

Partner Interview

- 'Buying a new car is the worst investment you can make; a car loses half its value as soon as you drive it out of the dealership.' Do you agree or disagree?
- Which country do you think makes the best luxury cars? Which country do you think makes the best budget cars?
- Do you negotiate with car dealers? Give an example of something you negotiated. Were you successful?
- What kind of car do you think we will drive when oil finally runs out? Which technology will win out in the end?

Consolidation

Ask a classmate what is most important to them when buying a new car? Safety? Style? Features? Brand? Price? Speed? Emissions?

Report your partner's priorities to the class and explain why your partner thinks these things are important.

Change and Transitions

Warm-up

How has your life changed in the last 10 years? What have been the biggest changes? Did you find the changes easy or difficult?

Key Vocabulary

transition / to adapt / to relocate / to get used to something / to keep up (with a changing world) / flexible / inflexible / likely / probable

Teacher → Pupil Questions

- Have you ever changed jobs? How long did it take you to adapt to your new role?
- How have your responsibilities at work changed since you started working?
- Have you ever quit your job?
- Have you ever changed careers? How did you manage this transition?
- Can you describe your transition from school/university to your first job?

Speaking activity

Imagine you have won the lottery. Make a short list of (a) what you would change in your life and (b) what you wouldn't change.

Swap lists with a partner. Ask your partner questions about their list. Explain *your* list to them.

Partner Interview

- Have you ever relocated/moved to a new city? What did you have to get used to?
- Do you find it easy or difficult to adapt to new situations? Give an example.
- Do you ever worry that you will become less flexible as you get older?
- Do you ever feel the world/technology is changing so fast that it's difficult to keep up?
- 'A change is as good as a rest.' What has been the most positive change you have ever made?

Consolidation

Write a list of what you think will be the 5 biggest changes the world will see in the next 50 years.

Then compare with a partner and discuss which changes on your two lists are most likely to happen. Put the list in order from most likely to least likely.

Report to the class and explain why you ordered the list the way you did.

Childhood

Warm-up

What was the best thing about being a child? What was the worst thing? Was your town/city/area a good place to grow up? Why/why not?

Key Vocabulary

to be the eldest / (school) subjects / to be in between / to regret (I wish I had/hadn't…) / experiences / talents / interests / peers / peer group

Teacher → Pupil Questions

- What school subjects were you good at as a child? Which were you not so good at?
- Did you used to enjoy school as a child? What were the positives and negatives?
- Were you the eldest child, the youngest child or 'in between' in your family? What did this mean for you and how did it affect you?
- Which experiences from childhood have been most important in making you who you are today?
- How has life changed since you were a child? Has it changed for the better or for the worse?

Speaking activity

Ask a partner: Do you have any regrets about the past? Is there any anything you wish you had done (or wish you hadn't done!)?

Report your partner's responses to the class.

Partner Interview

- Who was your biggest role model as a child? Why?
- What were your talents and interests as a child? Do you have any similar interests now?
- Which game did you enjoy most as a child?
- Which peer groups did you belong to during your childhood and teenage years?
- How did other children in your school class characterise you? The clown, the outsider, Mr popular, the intellectual, the hard-working one, the sporty one, et cetera?

Consolidation

With a partner, discuss how childhood today is different from when you were growing up. What experiences do children have today that you didn't have and vice versa? Think about education, technology, free time activities and childcare.

Report your partner's responses to the class.

Cities

Warm-up

What do you like most about living in your city/town? What do you dislike? What would you change about your city/town if you had the chance?

Key Vocabulary

urban / rural / suburban / inner-city / countryside / environment / convenient

Teacher → Pupil Questions

- Which city in the world did you enjoy visiting the most? Why?
- Which city would you most like to live in? Why?
- Which city in the world would you most like to visit? Why?
- What are the most important industries in your city? Are they important to the people that live there?

Speaking activity

Discuss briefly with a partner: What do you think cities will be like in the future? What do you think will change?

Report your ideas to the class.

Partner Interview

- Do you prefer living in the city or the countryside? What are the advantages and disadvantages?
- What do you find convenient about living in your city? Is there anything you find inconvenient?
- How was your city different in the past? Has it changed for the better?
- What do you look for in a city that you wish to live in? Low crime level? Good transportation? Beautiful architecture? Great shopping?

Consolidation

If you were elected mayor of your city, what changes would you make? Write down your ideas and present them to the class.

Mock election: Based on your classmate's ideas/presentations, who would you elect to be mayor of your city? Why?

Share your reasons with the class.

Communication

Warm-up

Is it important to be a good communicator in your profession? Do you think that people who communicate well are more successful? Which means of communication do you prefer?

Key Vocabulary

a means of communication / to relate (to people) / to rely on / to get in touch with someone / to get back to someone

Teacher → Pupil Questions

- Do you think the younger generation communicates differently than the older generation?
- Which means of communication to you find most efficient?
- Has the way you communicate changed in the last 20 years?
- Do you think people communicated more personally in the past?

Speaking activity

With a partner, discuss the advantages and disadvantages of communicating by a) telephone, b) email, c) SMS, d) instant message, d) video conferencing.

Share your ideas with the class.

Partner Interview

- Have you ever had trouble communicating with someone at work or in your private life? Tell the story.
- How has communication changed in the last 100 years?
- How do you think communication will change in the future?
- Do people who communicate a lot via social media find it difficult to relate to people interpersonally?
- How much is communicated through body language? Is it something you can rely on?

Consolidation

What do you think makes an effective communicator?

You and a partner have been asked to write a list of dos and don'ts for an upcoming book entitled *Communicating Effectively in Presentations*

Present your list to the class and explain why you think the points you included are important.

Commuting

Warm-up

How do you commute to your place of work? How far do you travel and how long does it take? What do you dislike most about commuting? The time? The expense? The energy?

Key Vocabulary

rush hour / traffic jam / public transport / congestion / gridlock / to encourage (people to do something) / traffic report / car park / irritating / frustrating / to improve / to be stuck in traffic

Teacher → Pupil Questions

- Is it difficult to find parking in your town/city? Is it expensive?
- Do you commute during rush hour? What is the best way to avoid getting stuck in traffic jams?
- What was public transport like in your city in the past? How do you think it will change in future?
- If you were offered a better job with a better salary, would you be willing to commute further?

Speaking activity

With a partner, discuss and list the advantages and disadvantages of taking your own car as opposed to using public transport for commuting.

Report your ideas to the class.

Partner Interview

- How would you rate the public transport system in your town/city? What would you improve?
- If public transport in your town/city were free of charge, would you use it more often?
- Do you ever use your bicycle to commute? If not, what would encourage you to do so?
- Is it easy to ride a bicycle in your town/city?
- What are the pros and cons of using a bicycle for commuting?

Consolidation

You are part of a committee that makes decisions on traffic and public transport issues in your city. Today you are attending a brainstorming meeting to think of ideas as to how you can encourage commuters to take their bicycles and use public transport. The city has a serious traffic problem!

With a partner, come up with 5 ideas as to how you could encourage commuters to take public transport / use their bicycles.

Then compare your list with another group's list. Decide on the 5 best suggestions from your 10 points. Share your ideas with the class.

Cooking

Warm-up

Are you a good cook? Why/why not? Which recipes do you cook most often? What is your favourite kind of food to cook? Why?

Key Vocabulary

to chop / to slice / to add (an ingredient) / to boil / to fry / to bake / to roast / to steam / to cube / to dice / to barbecue / starter / main course / dessert / course

Teacher → Pupil Questions

- ❒ Which meal (breakfast/lunch/dinner) do you enjoy cooking most?
- ❒ Do you like cooking as a social activity?
- ❒ Who do you like to cook with?
- ❒ Are you interested in cooking food from other cultures? Which cultures and why?
- ❒ What personal qualities and skills do you need to be a good cook, in your opinion?

Speaking activity

You and a partner want to write a cookery book.

Discuss: If you wrote a cookery book, what would it be called, what kind of food would it be and what would be your book's unique selling point?

Present your ideas to the class.

Partner Interview

- ❒ Are you interested in cookery programmes or celebrity chefs? Which celebrity chefs do you recommend? Which do you not recommend?
- ❒ Would you ever consider becoming a professional cook? What are the advantages and disadvantages of this profession?
- ❒ Describe your dream kitchen.
- ❒ 'Women are better cooks than men, simply because they are able to multitask!' Do you agree or disagree?

Consolidation

Explain to a partner how to cook one of your favourite recipes. First describe the ingredients needed and then how to prepare the food.

Cultural Differences

Warm-up

How does your culture compare to British [insert English-speaking country as needed] culture? What are the similarities and differences? Which cultural differences surprise you most when you are abroad?

Key Vocabulary

foreign / abroad / similarities / differences / to associate something with a culture / to adapt / rude / polite / to be surprised / values

Teacher → Pupil Questions

- Are there advantages to marrying someone from a different culture? Are there any disadvantages?
- Which foreign culture do you find especially interesting? Why?
- How do people from other countries see your culture? What is their first association?
- For what is your culture famous?

Speaking activity

Which values are especially important in your culture? Write down the 3 values you feel are the most important in your country. Then explain to a classmate why these values are important.

Share your partner's responses with the class.

Partner Interview

- What advice about cultural differences would you give someone who wanted to move to your country from abroad?
- Is it important to adapt to the culture of the country you are visiting/living in?
- Do you think it is important to regulate the number of immigrants coming into a country? Why/why not?
- What is considered rude in your country that is polite in other countries?
- Have you ever been surprised by the actions of someone from another culture?

Consolidation

You are attending the first meeting of a club you have just joined – The International Culture and Travel Club. The club organises trips to foreign countries for it's culture-hungry members. Tonight is a cocktail party to welcome and meet new members!

Stand up, circulate and ask the other new members (your classmates!) about the most interesting countries they have visited. What cultural differences did they notice?

Customer Service

Warm-up

Have you ever had to deal with a customer complaint? What happened? What is the best way to deal with a complaining customer, in your opinion? Would you like to work in a department that dealt with customer complaints? Why/why not?

Key Vocabulary

patience / to listen / understanding / empathy / to solve a problem / to return a product

Teacher → Pupil Questions

- Which types of businesses have the best customer service? Which have the worst?
- Do you think customer service is better or worse than it was 20 years ago?
- What is your opinion of customer service hotlines? Have you ever called such a hotline?
- Do you think more and more companies will use call-centres and hotlines in the future?
- Do you think people who work in customer service should be specially trained?

Speaking activity

Share your customer service experiences with a partner. With which businesses have you had good experiences? Which experiences have been bad?

Report to the class if either of you have had the same (or similar) experiences with a particular company.

Partner Interview

- What are the best/worst qualities for someone to have if they work in customer service?
- Does your company have a good customer service department?
- What do you think is the key to providing good customer service?
- Do you think customer service is better or worse in other countries?
- Have you ever returned a product you had bought? What happened? Tell the story.

Consolidation

Your boss has asked you to create some guidelines for how employees should deal with customer complaints in your company. Your recommendations should help employees to make customers feel heard and resolve the problem as soon as possible. Your goal is to have the customer return to your company in the future.

With a partner, create 5 guidelines and share them with the class.

CVs/Résumés

Warm-up

Are you very career orientated? Do you constantly try to improve your CV? How? What are CVs like in your country? Are they different to CVs from English speaking countries?

Key Vocabulary

personal qualities / skills / able to / capable of / education / qualifications / experience / field

Teacher → Pupil Questions

- Do you put a photo of yourself on your CV? What are the pros and cons of doing so?
- Do you think it is a good idea to put your age and gender on a CV? Why/why not?
- 'No one is ever as perfect as they are on their CV.' Are you completely honest on your CV?
- What is it important to have on your CV for a job specifically in your field?

Speaking activity

Jot down which 'personal qualities' (e.g. hard-working, loyal, patient, good communicator etc.) you think are needed for your profession.

Then write down your skills by completing the three sentences below:
- I can...
- I am able to...
- I am capable of...

Ask a partner to describe their personal qualities and skills to you. Report to the class.

Partner Interview

- What do you think is important for making a good layout for a CV?
- What do you think is more important to emphasise on a CV, qualifications or experience?
- Do you tailor your CV to individual jobs? Is this important? Do you find this time-consuming?
- Have you ever had to evaluate CVs and decide who would be invited to an interview? How did you find this experience? What made you invite the people you did?

Consolidation

With a partner, come up with a list of the top 5 dos and don'ts for writing a CV.

Compare your list with another group's list. Discuss and agree on the 'definitive' top 5 dos and don'ts.

Decisions

Warm-up

Would you like a job in which you had to make important decisions regularly? Do you have a strategy or method for making important decisions?

Key Vocabulary

to make a decision / decisive / indecisive / to have second thoughts / to regret / to change your mind / consequences / rational / irrational

Teacher → Pupil Questions

- ❒ Do you have to make decisions at work? How are good business decisions made?
- ❒ Who do you ask for advice before making important decisions?
- ❒ Have you ever made a decision and regretted it later?
- ❒ Have you ever made a big decision and then changed your mind/had second thoughts?

Speaking activity

A friend of yours calls you and asks you to lend him $5000 for a down payment on an apartment. Your friend's marriage has recently ended and it has hit your friend hard. You heard from your friend's ex-wife that he has a drug problem, which has gotten worse since the marriage ended.

With a partner, discuss what you would do in this situation. Then report to the class.

Partner Interview

- ❒ Can you think of a situation in which you had to make a tough decision?
- ❒ What is the hardest decision you've ever had to make? How did you make the decision?
- ❒ Are you good at making decisions or are you usually indecisive? Give an example.
- ❒ Which situations/jobs do you think require quick decision makers? Which situations benefit from considering all options slowly?
- ❒ Have you ever made a decision that had negative consequences?

Consolidation

You are a surgeon working in a large Accident and Emergency department. Your line manager (the head surgeon) has been behaving strangely in the last few weeks. He has been late for surgery several times and has had some sudden mood swings. The other day you noticed that he took some pills before he started an operation. Yesterday he almost gave a patient the wrong drug. Luckily you noticed in time. You tried to talk to him about it, but he became irritated and you backed off.

With a partner, discuss the situation and decide what to do.

Emergencies and Accidents

Warm-up

Have you ever had an accident at home / at work / on holiday / doing sports? What happened? How did the doctors treat you? How long did it take you to recover?

Key Vocabulary

to be accident prone / injury / bruise / to slip / to trip / ambulance / unconscious / to bleed / to panic / to examine / to break a bone / x-ray / lawyer / judge / witness / court / (his) fault

Teacher → Pupil Questions
- Are you a very accident-prone person?
- Does your employer take any steps to prevent accidents? Is health and safety a priority?
- Have you ever broken a bone? What happened?
- Are you good at giving first-aid?
- Do you think you would be a good person to be with in an emergency?

Speaking activity

Test your 'First Aid IQ.' With a partner, discuss what you would do in the following situations:
- Someone is bleeding from a wound
- You think someone has broken their leg
- Someone is choking
- Someone is unconscious but breathing
- Someone has burnt their arm with boiling water

Report to the class and discuss any differences of opinion.

Partner Interview
- Have you ever been involved in a road traffic accident? What happened?
- What injuries did you have?
- Was there much damage to the car(s)?
- Where there any witnesses?
- Whose fault was the accident?
- Did you have to go to court?
- What did the judge decide in the end?

Consolidation: Role Play

Role A: You are jogging with a friend when your companion falls and hits his head quite badly. He is unconscious and you cannot tell if he is breathing or not. You have never done a first aid course. Call an ambulance and ask what you can do to help until the ambulance arrives.
Role B: You are a paramedic. You have just been called to deal with an accident victim that has

had a bad fall. However, you are 20 minutes away from the location of the accident. In such situations, you sometimes give first aid advice to people at the scene of the accident over the phone. Your phone is ringing. Answer it.

Employment

Warm-up

Do you find it easy or difficult to divide your time between leisure and work? How many hours work per week would you find ideal? Which kind of job suits you best? Why?

Key Vocabulary

employment prospects / abroad / to emigrate / conditions of work / commitment

Teacher → Pupil Questions

- Do you prefer working on your own or with other people?
- Do you prefer to work with computers or in a more social role, such as in a team?
- Which companies offer the best employment prospects, in your opinion?
- Would you look for work abroad if there were no work in your home country? Where would you go? What kind of work would you look for?
- Do people from your country typically emigrate to find work abroad? Where do they go?

Speaking activity

Quickly jot down a few pros and cons of each job you have done so far in your life.

Then compare your positives and negatives with what a classmate has written down. Ask if they also see your positives as advantages and your negatives as disadvantages.

Share your opinions with the class.

Partner Interview

- What positive effects does working have on your life? E.g. Wealth, a sense of purpose etc. Are there any negative consequences? E.g. Stress, less time for family etc.
- What conditions of work do you find acceptable? Which would you find unacceptable?
- Have you ever had difficulty finding employment?
- What do you think would be the worst thing about being unemployed?
- 'Unemployed people should be forced to accept *any* job that is available, even if it is badly paid.' Do you agree or disagree?

Consolidation

Are you very committed to your company? If yes, what does the company *do* that gives you this sense of commitment? If not, what *could* the company do to increase your commitment?

Stand up, circulate and ask each of your classmates how committed they are to their company (or a company they worked for in the past). In each case, find out the *reasons* for the person's level of commitment.

Share and discuss: What were the most common reasons for a high level of commitment? What were the most common reasons for a low level of commitment?

Entrepreneurs

Warm-up

Are entrepreneurs encouraged in your country? Does the government support entrepreneurs in any way? In which areas do the people from your county have entrepreneurial spirit? Do you?

Key Vocabulary

entrepreneur / entrepreneurial spirit / passion / niche / pressure / reward / profit / risk / start-up

Teacher → Pupil Questions

- What are the biggest growth-industries the moment? Which would you choose if you wanted to start a business?
- What are the advantages/disadvantages of being an entrepreneur?
- Which entrepreneur do you admire the most?
- Do you think 'Entrepreneur-ship' should be a subject that is taught at school?

Speaking activity

Discuss briefly with a partner: What advice would you give someone interested in starting their own business? What do you think is important?

Report your ideas to the class.

Partner Interview

- Would you like to start your own business? What kind of business would it be?
- 'Profit is the reward for risk.' Do you agree or disagree?
- Are you good at handling risk and insecurity?
- Is it difficult to find a profitable niche in this day and age?
- More and more jobs are being done by computers and machines. Which industries do you think are future proof?

Consolidation

Which character traits do you need to start and run a business successfully? Prioritise the following list, starting with the trait you think is most important. Explain your choices to the class.

- Passion and enthusiasm
- Skill and expertise
- Ability to learn from your mistakes
- Ability to handle pressure and risk

Environment

Warm-up

How does the state of the environment in your country compare to other countries? Have you noticed any weather or climate changes in your country in recent years? What does your government do to encourage people to take care of the environment?

Key Vocabulary

alternative energy / to be aware of something / environmental awareness / attitudes / sources (of energy) / global warming / environmentally friendly / laws / community

Teacher → Pupil Questions

- Is your company very aware of environmental issues? In what ways?
- Is the environment an important issue for people in your country compared to other countries?
- Do you think the actions of a single person can make a difference?
- Do you recycle? If so, what do you recycle and how?
- Would you consider driving a hybrid or electric car? Why/why not?
- Have attitudes towards the environment changed since you were a child? How?

Speaking activity

With a partner, list the advantages and disadvantages of alternative energy sources. Which do you think look most promising and why?

Present your ideas to the class.

Partner Interview

- Do strict environmental laws make industries in such countries uncompetitive?
- What do you think is most important: caring for the environment (a) at an individual level, (b) at a community level, (c) at a governmental level or (d) at an industrial level?
- Which energy sources are most used in your country? Is your country dependent on other countries for its energy?
- Do you think nuclear power is the answer to the energy problem or do you think it is too dangerous to consider?

Consolidation

Create a questionnaire of 5 questions to discover how 'green' your classmates are. Survey your classmates to find out who is the most environmentally friendly person in the class.

Report to the class why this person is the 'greenest.'

Ethical Eating

Warm-up

How do you choose the food you eat? Do ethical and environmental concerns play a role? Do you find it difficult to know if your food has been produced ethically?

Key Vocabulary

humane / well-treated / badly-treated / battery farming / to produce / consumer

Teacher → Pupil Questions

- Do you think it is wrong to raise and kill animals for humans to eat?
- If the process is humane, does that make a difference?
- Do you think animals should have rights?
- Do you try to eat food that is grown locally? Should we try to eat less food that is transported from far away countries?
- What is your opinion of battery farming?

Speaking activity

With a partner, discuss which of the following foods is the most ethical food to eat and which is the least ethical. Put the list in order, starting with the most ethical food and ending with the least ethical.

- Farmed salmon
- Eggs from a battery farm
- Beef from Argentina
- Corn that has been genetically modified to repel insects

Share with the class and tell the class why you chose the order you did.

Partner Interview

Discuss the following facts with a partner. Report your partner's reactions to the class.

- 2400 gallons of water are needed to produce 1 pound (454g) of beef.
- One-sixth of an acre of land can feed a vegetarian for a year. Over 3 acres are needed to feed the equivalent meat eater.
- It takes up to 13 pounds of grain to produce just 1 pound of meat.
- Fish on fish farms must be fed up to 5 pounds of wild fish to produce 1 pound of farmed fish.
- It takes more than 11 times as much fossil fuel to make one calorie from animal protein as it does to make one calorie from plant protein.
- A large percentage of land used to farm animals is cleared forestland.

Consolidation

Prepare 3 arguments *for* or *against* the following statement:

'Only meat that is ethically produced should be allowed. The cost should be passed on to the consumer.'

Share and discuss with the class.

Family Life

Warm-up

What were the most important values in your family when you were growing up? Is your country very 'family friendly?'

Key Vocabulary

to get along (with someone) / values / roles / influence / day care / to look after (children) / to take care of (children)

Teacher → Pupil Questions

- How did your family's values influence you? Were there any values you rejected?
- What values would you like to pass on to your children?
- How do you think family life has changed in the last 30 years?
- How do you think family life will change in the future in your country?

Speaking activity

'Families take so many forms these days: families in which the father and mother are unmarried, single-parent families, families with same-sex parents, families in which the father stays at home with the children. It's time to rethink our definition of family.'

With a partner, write a definition of the word *family*. What does the word family mean to you? Share.

Partner Interview

- Did your parents have very traditional roles (i.e. father as the breadwinner, mother staying at home with the children, et cetera)?
- Do you think these roles are changing? What is the situation in your country?
- Do you think it is better for children to go to day care institutions with lots of other children or is it better for the child to stay at home?
- Do you think the state should pay for day care institutions, so that more parents can work?
- At what age do you think a child is ready to go to day care?

Consolidation: Debate

With a group or partner, write 3 of arguments *for* or *against* the following:

'Some women feel guilty for being more career focused and less family focused. Some men feel 'useless' when staying at home to care for children. The 'traditional' conception of the family leads to happier families.'

Fashion

Warm-up

What is your favourite brand of clothing? Why? Do the people in your country have their own sense of fashion? How does it compare to other countries?

Key Vocabulary

to be fashion conscious / to make a fashion statement / brand / in vogue / in fashion / out of fashion / trends / to express oneself / fashion sense / similar / different

Teacher → Pupil Questions

- What kind of clothes do you usually wear?
- How important is it to you to be fashionably dressed?
- Do you feel differently about yourself when you are well dressed?
- Do you ever feel under pressure to be fashionably dressed?
- Are you very fashion conscious?

Speaking activity

What trends have you noticed that are in vogue at the moment? Write down a few thoughts.

Then compare with a partner and ask if they have noticed the same trends.

Share your results with the class.

Partner Interview

- Which trends that are fashionable at the moment do you think will disappear in 6 months?
- What is your opinion of the fashion industry?
- Do you think fashion repeats itself? Can you think of any examples?
- Do you think you can express yourself/your personality through what you wear?
- What do you think makes a bigger fashion statement: wearing clothes that are similar to what most people wear or wearing clothes that are different?

Consolidation

With a partner, compare fashions from the eighties, nineties, naughties and current fashions. Discuss and list which clothes you think epitomised (were typical of) each decade.

Then compare your ideas with another group's ideas. Share the similarities and differences with the class.

Festivals and Celebrations

Warm-up

Which festivals/celebrations do you most enjoy? What activities normally take place at these festivals? If you could visit any festival in the world, which one would it be and why?

Key Vocabulary

attractions / atmosphere / to take place / advertisement / slogan / festival

Teacher → Pupil Questions

- Have you ever attended an arts, music or theatre festival?
- Describe the atmosphere. What were the highlights?
- What festivals take place in your city or hometown?
- Are there special foods at this celebration? Do you give gifts?
- Where and how did this festival originate?

Speaking activity

You are seriously considering visiting a festival for your vacation this year, since you would like to try something different. Ask a partner if they can recommend a festival they have visited in the past. What were the positives and negatives?

Report to the class if you would visit the festival based on your partner's recommendation.

Partner Interview

- Which festivals did you celebrate as child?
- Which festivals do you celebrate with friends, which with family?
- Do you celebrate the New Year in your country? How do you celebrate it?
- Describe your last New Year's celebration.
- Do you follow any customs at New Year?

Consolidation

You manage the local tourist board. With a classmate, make an advertisement for a local festival. Include the following:

- A catchy slogan
- 3 notable attractions or benefits (in bullet points)
- A special offer to attract visitors

Your aim is to attract people to the festival to support local businesses. Share with the class.

First Impressions

Warm-up

What is the first thing you notice when you meet someone new? What do you think is most important when trying to make a good impression? To smile? To maintain eye contact? To be yourself?

Key Vocabulary

to make a good impression / interview / to get to know someone / personality / appearances can be deceptive / to come across well / to be well dressed

Teacher → Pupil Questions

- Do you think it is possible to teach someone how to make a good first impression?
- What impression did you have of your partner the first time you met?
- Have you ever had a bad first impression of someone and then changed your mind when you got to know them better?
- 'The most important thing is to be yourself.' Do you agree?

Speaking activity

What kind of first impression do you think *you* make on other people? Tell your partner and ask if they agree with you. What was your partner's first impression of you?

Partner Interview

- Do you make first impressions based on how well someone is dressed?
- Have you ever made a bad first impression? Tell the story.
- On which occasions is it most important to make a good first impression?
- 'Appearances can be deceptive.' Do you agree?
- 'First impressions last.' Do you agree?

Consolidation

In your opinion, what are the 5 best tips for making a good impression at a job interview?

Come up with the 5 tips that you think are most important.

Compare your list with another student's list. Discuss and try to agree on the 5 best tips from the 10 you now have in front of you. Put them in order from most important to least important.

Share with the class.

Food

Warm-up

It is often said that breakfast is the most important meal of the day. Do you think this is true? Which meal do you think is most important? What do you typically eat for breakfast?

Key Vocabulary

eating habits / organic / speciality / to be a fussy eater / to prepare (food) / ingredients / to slice / to chop / to stir / to peel / to mix / to boil / to bake / to roast / to fry / to steam / to grill

Teacher → Pupil Questions

- What are your eating habits?
- Do you like to eat fast food? What are the pros and cons?
- Do you like to eat organic food? What are the pros and cons?
- Do you think organic food is too expensive?
- What is your national dish? What ingredients does it have? Is it eaten at a special time of year? How is it prepared? What is it usually served with?

Speaking activity

Stand up, circulate and find out whose eating preferences are *most similar* to your own.

Then report to the class what you have in common with that person. Include both likes and dislikes.

Partner Interview

- What is the speciality of your region? Would you recommend it to visitors?
- What is your favourite international cuisine?
- 'You are what you eat.' Do you agree?
- Are you a fussy eater? Do you know anybody who is a fussy eater?
- What kinds of foods did you used to hate as a child that you now enjoy?
- Have there been any food scares in your country in the last few years? What happened? Did it change your eating habits?

Consolidation

Write a quick recipe for your favourite meal. Include a list of ingredients as well as some instructions on how to prepare the meal.

Explain to a partner how to cook your favourite meal.

Friends

Warm-up

What do you have in common with your good friends? What do you not have in common? Do you have any friends that only talk about themselves? Do you consider these people real friends?

Key Vocabulary

friendship / to have things in common / lifelong friends / character / appearance / sense of humour / connection

Teacher → Pupil Questions

- Have you ever made any friends on the Internet? If so, how? If not, would you ever consider doing this?
- Do you have any friends you consider lifelong-friends? What made your friendship so deep?
- Do you have any friends that only ever tell you about their problems?
- Do you think good friends need to have a lot in common, or do you think people who have different interests can be good friends?
- What is the best environment in which to make new friends? School? Work? Clubs?

Speaking activity

Ask a partner to compare two of their good friends. In what ways are they similar/different? Ask about character, appearance, interests, sense of humour, likes and dislikes.

Share your partner's comparison with the class.

Partner Interview

- In your opinion, what is the secret to keeping a friendship alive?
- Did you find it easier to make new friends when you were younger?
- Do you think it is possible for men and women to just be friends?
- Opinion 1: 'Friends take time and energy. That's why I only have a few good friends.' Opinion 2: 'Friends give you lots of energy. That's why I have lots of them!' Which opinion do you agree with more?
- Do you think of Facebook friends (or contacts from other social media platforms) as 'real' friends?

Consolidation

Discuss with a partner: How do you think female friendships are different to male friendships?

Report your ideas to the class.

Future Predictions

Warm-up

Where do you see yourself in 10 years? Are you optimistic or pessimistic about the future? Why? In what ways do you think life will be better in the future? In what ways will it be worse?

Key Vocabulary

to predict / to change for the better / likely / unlikely / technology / advances / to develop / to progress (v.) / progression / to prevent

Teacher → Pupil Questions

- How do you think the cars of the future will be different to today?
- How do you think your country will change in the future?
- Which countries do you think will be superpowers in 50 years?
- What will the world's biggest problem be in the next 50 years?

Speaking activity

Discuss with a partner: What changes do you think will happen in the following areas in the next 100 years?

- Health care
- Energy production
- Houses
- Education
- Computers and related devices (smartphones, wearable devices etc.)
- Transport

Partner Interview

- How did you imagine the future when you were younger? Did any of the things you imagined become reality?
- Which new industries will exist in 50 years time? Which will no longer exist?
- Which jobs will no longer exist in 50 years time?
- Do you think life will be easier or more difficult for our children? How?

Consolidation

Discuss with a partner: How likely are the following statements, in your opinion. Rate each statement either (a) very likely, (b) possible or (c) very unlikely and give reasons for your answers.

Within the next 50 years...

- School children will only use tablets in school. Books will be a thing of the past.

- Space tourism will be a reality, not only for the super-rich.
- We will pay using our mobile phones. Cash will no longer exist.
- 50% of CEOs and senior politicians will be women.
- There will be another world war.

Report your ideas to the class and share why you think each statement is likely or unlikely.

Gaming

Warm-up

Are you a gamer? How much do you enjoy computer games? How much time do you spend playing? What genre of video game (shooters, role-play, war, adventure etc.) do you enjoy most?

With a partner, brainstorm as many game genres you can think of in 2 minutes.

Key Vocabulary

device / to compare / games console / the object of the game / skill / ability / to complete / to defeat / to complete (a level) / to explore / to interact / to control

Teacher → Pupil Questions

- Which device do you prefer for playing computer games? Handheld, PC, games console?
- What makes a good computer game, in your opinion?
- Which games are popular at the moment? Why do you think they are popular?
- Do you like to play computer games alone or with friends?
- Do you prefer 2-D or 3-D games?

Speaking activity

Make a list of your top 3 games of all time. Then compare your list with the partners list. Discuss and agree on the 'definitive' top 3 games.

Present your final list to the class and say *why* these games made it onto the list.

Partner Interview

- Compare the last 2 computer games you played. What were the positives and negatives?
- How have computer games changed in the last 20 years?
- How do you think computer games will change in the future?
- What is/was your parents' attitude to computer games?
- What are the advantages of using a games console designed specially for playing games?
- Do you like to play online games? What are the advantages of playing online?

Consolidation

Ask a partner to think of a video game they have played that they think is *good*, but not *excellent*. Ask them why they would not give the game full marks. Then ask them to describe how they would improve the game to make it 'excellent.'

Report your partner's ideas to the class.

Gender Roles

Warm-up

In your country, are the roles of men and women in the family very different? Do you think the education system pushes boys and girls in different directions? What was your own experience?

Key Vocabulary

expectations / stereotypes / messy / disorganised / to be obsessed with something / gender-neutral / traditional / preschool (day care)

Teacher → Pupil Questions

- How are gender roles different in other countries you have visited?
- Do you think boys are raised with different expectations to girls and vice versa?
- Girls consistently outperform boys in school. Are girls simply more intelligent than boys?
- Boys and girls often play with different toys. Girls frequently play with dolls and boys with cars. Do you think this is because they naturally prefer different toys or because they are given different ones?

Speaking activity

Brainstorm with a partner: In which areas of life is it easier to be a man? In which areas is it easier to be a woman?

Share your ideas with the class.

Partner Interview

- 'Men are terrible at multitasking and women can't read maps.' Is any truth in these stereotypes?
- 'Men are disorganized. Women are obsessed with cleaning.' Do you agree or disagree?
- Boys are often given blue, brown and other dark coloured clothing; girls are given pink, white and other light coloured clothing. What effect do you think this has?

Consolidation

In 2011, the first gender-neutral day care preschool opened in Stockholm. In this school, teachers avoid using the pronouns 'him' and 'her', books are carefully chosen to avoid traditional presentations of gender roles and children play with whatever toys they want, including toys intended for the other gender.

Pair work: What is your opinion of this idea? Would you send your child to a gender-neutral preschool?

Gender Roles in the Workplace

Warm-up

Do you think women have equal opportunities in your country? Are women paid the same as men? Is it as easy for a woman to get a promotion as it is for a man?

Key Vocabulary

workplace / opportunities / promotion / glass ceiling / breadwinner / homemaker

Teacher → Pupil Questions

- What are typical male professions where you come from? What are typical female professions? Are the female professions less well paid?
- Have you noticed a 'glass ceiling' in your company?
- Would you rather work for a male or female boss? Why?
- If you were a boss, would you prefer a male or female assistant? Why?
- Are there laws in your country that try to create equality between men and women?

Speaking activity

With a partner, make a list of 5 ways that male and female roles have changed in the last 30 years. Discuss briefly how these roles might change in the *next* 30 years?

Report your ideas to the class.

Partner Interview

- Is it easy for women continue their careers after starting a family in your country?
- In so-called traditional societies, men are the breadwinners and women are the homemakers. Do you think these roles are out-dated or do you think the traditional way is best?
- If you are a man, would you be willing to stay at home with young children while your partner went out to work?
- If you are a woman, would you be willing to be the breadwinner while your partner stayed at home with the children?

Consolidation

Do men or women mainly do the following jobs: (a) kindergarten teacher, (b) soldier, (c) nurse, (d) engineer?

Class discussion: Do you think that men and women are drawn to different professions because of their *nature*, or do you think society *expects* men and women to enter certain professions?

Globalisation

Warm-up

Do you try to 'buy local' or do you enjoy having more choice in the global marketplace? Has globalisation had a positive or negative impact on your country/business? How?

Key Vocabulary

consumer / global / to compete / competition / competitor / labour market / abroad / local / domestic / outsourcing / global inequality / to do business

Teacher → Pupil Questions

- Do you know any companies that have had to close because of competition from abroad?
- Does your company face tough competition from other global companies?
- Which technologies help a company to operate globally?
- Does the food you eat come from further away than it did 20 years ago? What about the clothes you wear?

Speaking activity

Which jobs do you think will still exist in your country in 20 years? Which do you think will be done in another country? Discuss with a partner and make a list of your ideas.

Share with the class.

Partner Interview

- 'I love living in a globalised world. Prices are cheaper and I have a larger choice of products.' How do you benefit from globalisation?
- 'It is impossible for small companies to compete in a globalised world.' What is your opinion?
- 'Globalisation is bad for the environment – we don't need our food flown half way around the world before it lands on our dinner plate.' Do you agree?
- 'The only way to stop your job being outsourced to a second or third world country is to have specialist knowledge and make yourself indispensible.' Do you agree?
- Do you think globalisation increases 'global fairness' or 'global inequality?'

Consolidation

Work is increasingly being outsourced to cheaper labour markets. With a partner, write a list of the advantages and disadvantages of outsourcing. In your opinion, do the advantages outweigh the disadvantages?

Share your ideas with the class.

Habits

Warm-up

What habits do you have at work? Do you have any habits that make you more productive? Do you have any habits that make you *less* productive at work?

Key Vocabulary

to pick up (a habit) / to give something up / always / frequently / usually / often / effective

Teacher → Pupil Questions

- What are your good habits?
- Do you have any bad habits?
- What are your eating habits?
- Describe your exercise habits.
- Do you have any habits that you would like to change?

Speaking activity

Talk with a partner and try to find out which habits you have in common.

Share your common habits with the class.

Partner Interview

- Describe the habits of a member of your family.
- Do any members of your family have habits that annoy you?
- Which habits do you think are important for children to learn?
- Which habits did you pick up as a child? Which habits didn't you pick up?

Consolidation

There is a popular book entitled *7 Habits of Highly Effective People*. In your opinion, what habits do highly effective people have? Make a short list.

Compare your list with a partner's list and share the differences with the class.

Having Children

Warm-up

Is your country very family friendly? Is it easy to raise children where you come from? Is it easy for parents to stop work to start a family in your country? Is this harder for men or for women?

Key Vocabulary

IVF treatment / day care / an only child / exhausting / to feel guilty / to be a provider / advice / to encourage / to discourage

Teacher → Pupil Questions

- What is the cost of childcare where you come from? Are there enough day care places?
- How many children is the ideal number, in your opinion?
- What do you think is better for children: to be an only child, to be a child in a small family, or to be a child with lots of brothers and sisters?
- In developed countries the trend is towards smaller families. What are the pros and cons?

Speaking activity

In 2008, a 70-year-old Indian woman gave birth to twins after having IVF treatment.

Discuss with a partner: Do you think there should be an age limit for having children? If so, what should it be? What is your opinion of people having children in their 50s and 60s with the help of modern medicine?

Present you ideas to the class.

Partner Interview

- 'Having children is both the most amazing experience and the most exhausting experience I've ever had.' If you have children, do you agree? If not, is this encouraging or discouraging?
- Do you think mothers are under social pressure to be the 'perfect' mother? Do many women feel guilty if they are working mothers?
- Do you think fathers are under social pressure to be the 'perfect' provider?
- Has the role of 'mother' changed in the last 50 years? Has the role of 'father' changed?

Consolidation

What advice would you give a young couple intending to have children? Circulate and tell your advice to your classmates.

Afterwards, tell the class who you think gave the best advice and why.

Health

Warm-up

Do you go to the doctor very often? How did you choose your doctor? What is your doctor like? Describe him/her.

Key Vocabulary

general practitioner (GP) / bedside manner / hypochondriac / health insurance / citizen / compulsory (health insurance) / (insurance) contributions / insurance policy / level of cover

Teacher → Pupil Questions

- Do you have any good habits when it comes to taking care of your health? Do you have any bad habits?
- Would you ever consider a career as a doctor? What do you think are the positive and negative things about being a doctor?
- What do you think is the most difficult part of the doctor's job?
- Do you know anyone who is a hypochondriac? How does this affect their life?

Speaking activity

Ask a partner to compare doctors they have been to in the past. What were the positives and negatives? Then, together with your partner, write a list of 5 points on what you think makes a good doctor.

Compare your list with another group's list and try and try to agree on the 'definitive' 5 points.

Partner Interview

- Is medical care in your country very expensive?
- Does your GP have a good 'bedside manner?'
- Which qualities do you think doctors need?
- Some doctors have been criticised for simply writing prescriptions to avoid treating the 'person behind the patient.' Do you think this is true?
- Some people say the drug industry is all about money. Do you agree or disagree?

Consolidation

In some countries, the state pays for citizens' medical care. In other countries, patients have to pay medical bills themselves, or have private health insurance.

Which system do you think is better? Discuss the advantages and disadvantages of each system and present your ideas to the class.

Healthy Living and Exercise

Warm-up

How do you take care of your health? Who is the healthiest person you know? What habits does this person have that make them so healthy, in your opinion?

Key Vocabulary

attitude / cardiovascular exercise / resistance training / diet / to maintain (your body) / to have a good figure / to keep in shape / to be out of shape

Teacher → Pupil Questions

- How frequently do you take exercise? What kind of exercise do you take?
- How important is good quality sleep in staying healthy, in your opinion?
- Would you describe your lifestyle as passive or active?
- Do you belong to a gym? What are the pros and cons?

Speaking activity

Discuss with a partner: Do you think men and women have different attitudes to healthy living and exercise?

Then make a list of the differences between men and women in terms of healthy living.

Share your ideas with the class.

Partner Interview

- What are the advantages and disadvantages of cardiovascular exercise versus resistance training? Which do you prefer?
- Which kind of exercise is the 'best' kind of exercise, in your opinion?
- Do you take exercise because you want to be healthy or to maintain a good figure?
- Have you ever been on a diet? Describe the experience. If not, would you ever consider going on a diet?

Consolidation

With a partner, create a list of the top 5 dos and don'ts for healthy living.

Compare your list with another group's list. Discuss and agree on the 'definitive' top 5 dos and don'ts.

Present your ideas to the class.

Healthy Eating

Warm-up

Which meal is the most important meal of the day, in your opinion? Do you think it is better to eat 3 large meals a day or to eat smaller meals more often? What are your eating habits?

Key Vocabulary

nutrition / nutrients / balanced diet / vitamins / minerals / supplements / carbohydrates / fats / proteins / fibre / to prevent / stimulants / caffeine

Teacher → Pupil Questions

- ❏ Which food do you think is the 'best' food? Which food deserves the name 'super-food?'
- ❏ What balance of carbohydrates, fats, proteins, and fibre do you think is ideal?
- ❏ How do you get vitamins and minerals? Do you take supplements?
- ❏ Do you look at the nutritional information on food packaging? What do you look out for?

Speaking activity

Discuss with a partner: Which of the following recipes do you think has following nutritional values: fat 10g (2g saturated fat), carbohydrate 26g, protein 31g, fibre 5g?

- Salmon with fennel, potato and pesto
- Chicken curry with rice, broccoli and coconut milk
- Carrot, orange and avocado salad with lettuce

Report your choice to the class and give reasons for your choice.

Partner Interview

- ❏ Do you think vitamin C really helps to prevent colds? Are there any other ways of preventing colds?
- ❏ Do you drink coffee and tea? How much of these stimulants do you think is healthy/unhealthy?
- ❏ Are your energy levels consistent throughout the day? Describe your biorhythm.
- ❏ Which foods keep your energy level constant? Which give you fast energy followed by a crash?
- ❏ Does anyone you know suffer from allergies? How do allergies affect their lifestyle?

Consolidation

Write a survey of 5 questions designed to find out which of your classmates has the healthiest diet. Circulate and survey the rest of your class to find out.

Share your results with the class and give your reasons.

Heroes and Heroines

Warm-up

Which famous person do you admire most in the world? Which walk of life do they come from (the stage, politics, music, et cetera)? Which people from your everyday life do you admire? Who is your hero? Why?

Key Vocabulary

idol / to idolise / to admire / to be enthusiastic about / role model / to look up to someone

Teacher → Pupil Questions

- Who was your hero when you were a child? What about when you were a teenager?
- Who was your role model when you were a child/teenager?
- Do you think people who are role models should act responsibly in public (professional football players, movie stars, etc.)?
- Would you like to be famous? What do you think are the pros and cons of being famous?

Speaking activity

If you could interview any person living or dead, who would it be and why?

Write down 3 reasons for your choice and tell the rest of the class.

Partner Interview

- Did you idolise any pop stars or sports figures as a teenager?
- Why do you think teenagers do this more intensively than older people?
- Are you a huge fan of a group, singer, actor or sportsperson? How do you express your enthusiasm for them?
- Who would you like your teenage children to have as their heroes? Who would you *not* like them to have? Why?

Consolidation

Write down 5 questions you would like to ask your hero.

Then imagine you *are* your hero. Give your questions to a classmate and let them interview you as your hero.

History

Warm-up

Did you enjoy studying history at school? Which countries' histories did you study? From which eras? Did you learn anything that was useful to you personally?

Key Vocabulary

period / era / historical figure / historical event / invention / insight

Teacher → Pupil Questions

- Do you think it is important to study history? Why/why not?
- Who do you think is the most important figure in your country's history?
- Which event in your country's history do you find most interesting?
- Do you think history repeats itself?

Speaking activity

Ask a partner: If you could go back in time and speak with any historical figure, who would it be and why? What would you ask them?

Report your partner's responses to the class.

Partner Interview

- If you could live in any historical period, which period would you choose and why?
- Do you think humans learn from their mistakes? Or do humans simply repeat the same mistakes over and over again?
- Have you ever read a historical novel or seen a movie set in a different time period? What was the book or film? Did it give you a good insight into life at the time it was set?
- Which events that are happening in the world at the moment do you think will be big events in tomorrow's history books? Why?

Consolidation

With a partner, make a list of what you think are the 5 most important inventions in History: the inventions that have changed our lives the most.

Compare your list with another group's list. Discuss and agree on the 'definitive' top 5 most important inventions in History.

Present your 'final' list to the class.

Hobbies

Warm-up

What is your favourite hobby? When and why did you take up this hobby? Are there any new hobbies you would you like to try? Why?

Key Vocabulary

to take up / to give something up / unusual / exotic / profession / to earn money

Teacher → Pupil Questions

- How often do you do your favourite hobby?
- What kind of person do you need to be for this hobby?
- What kind of equipment is needed for your hobby?
- What costs are involved in your hobby?
- What hobbies did you do in the past but don't do anymore? Why did you give them up?
- Do you know anyone with an exotic or unusual hobby?

Speaking activity

Ask a partner about their favourite hobby. What kind of person do you need to be to do this hobby? What skills, personal qualities or talents do you need to practice this hobby successfully?

Share your partner's responses with the class.

Partner Interview

- Do you know anyone with an expensive hobby?
- Are you someone who changes your hobbies often?
- Do you know anyone who doesn't have any hobbies? Do you think it's important to have hobbies?
- Do you know anyone who has made their hobby into their profession?
- Do you know anyone who earns money from their hobby?

Consolidation

Is it good for couples/partners to have the same hobbies?

Stand up, circulate and find out (a) who thinks this is a good thing and (b) who thinks this a bad thing.

What is the general consensus? Report your results to the class.

Holidays/Vacations

Warm-up

Which countries appeal to you as a holiday destination? Why? Which countries don't appeal to you?

Key Vocabulary

destination / active / passive / cruise / to appeal (to you) / scenery / sights / accommodation

Teacher → Pupil Questions

- Do you prefer active or passive holidays?
- Do you prefer sun-holidays or cold-weather holidays?
- Do you prefer to travel by train, plane, bus or car when going on holiday? Why?
- What activities do you like to do on holiday (hiking/surfing/sightseeing, et cetera)?
- How do family holidays differ from holidays without a family?

Speaking activity

Ask a partner to describe their best holiday or business trip. What made it so good?

Share your partner's responses with the class.

Partner Interview

- Which country that you have not yet visited would you like to go to on holiday? Why does that country appeal to you?
- Have you ever booked an all-inclusive holiday? What are the advantages/disadvantages?
- Have you ever taken a cruise? Does this kind of holiday appeal to you? Why/why not?
- Describe your worst holiday or business trip. What made it so bad?

Consolidation

Ask a partner to compare their last two holidays. Which was better and why? Ask about the following:

- Scenery
- Accommodation
- Weather
- People
- Sights
- Experiences

Report your partner's responses to the class.

Homes and Houses

Warm-up

What would you consider important if you were buying a new home? What would be your priorities? Describe your home. How many rooms do you have? What does your house look like?

Key Vocabulary

to rent / landlord / tenant / furnishings / furniture / to be house-proud / neighbourhood / area / location / view / convenient / inconvenient / detached / semi-detached / terraced house

Teacher → Pupil Questions

- Do you have a favourite room in your house? Why is it your favourite?
- What are the pros and cons of living in a house versus living in an apartment?
- Is it important to you to have a garden? Does gardening appeal to you as a hobby?
- Describe your neighbourhood. What are the positives and negatives?
- Are you a very house-proud person?

Speaking activity

Take a minute to think about what your dream home would look like. Consider the design, furnishings, style and location.

Describe your dream home to a classmate.

Partner Interview

- If you could change one thing about your home, what would it be?
- How do you think houses will change in the future?
- Are you happy with the location of your home?
- What do you look for when choosing a location for your home? What is most important to you?
- What is the most exclusive neighbourhood in your area? Would you like to live there? Why/why not?

Consolidation

Do you think it is better to rent a home or to buy?

With a partner, make a list of the advantages and disadvantages of renting versus buying a home. Does it depend on the housing market? Is this a better time to rent or to buy?

Report your ideas to the class.

Hometowns

Warm-up

Where is your hometown? What do you like/dislike about your hometown? How has your hometown changed since you were a child? Has it changed for the better or for the worse?

Key Vocabulary

city / town / village / landmark / event / festival / history / atmosphere / location / rural area / urban area / countryside / convenient / inconvenient

Teacher → Pupil Questions

- Would you like to live in your hometown or doesn't the idea appeal to you?
- Are there any are the local traditions in your hometown?
- Is your hometown famous for anything?
- What industries are present in your hometown? How important are they for the town or city?

Speaking activity

Imagine you are thinking of moving to your classmate's hometown. Ask him/her about the pros and cons of living there.

Would you move to your partner's hometown based on their description? Report to the class.

Partner Interview

- Do you celebrate any festivals in your hometown?
- Does your hometown have an interesting history?
- What are the main attractions in your hometown?
- Is your hometown growing? How do you think your hometown will change in the next 20 years?
- If you could change one thing in your hometown, what would you change?

Consolidation

Give your partner a 'verbal tour' of your hometown. Describe (a) one landmark, (b) one event and (c) one person and explain why they are important aspects of your hometown.

Honesty and Lying

Warm-up

Do you think it is okay to lie to avoid hurting someone's feelings? At what times do you appreciate people being honest with you?

Key Vocabulary

to tell a lie / liar / honest / dishonest / to be economical with the truth / to hurt someone's feelings / to cheat / to tell the truth / white lie / to justify something / to be brutally honest

Teacher → Pupil Questions

- ❐ Do you think white lies are acceptable?
- ❐ Is dishonesty ever justifiable? What about being economical with the truth?
- ❐ Has anyone ever been dishonest to you? Tell the story.
- ❐ 'A person is never as perfect as on their CV/résumé.' Are you 100% honest on your CV?
- ❐ Has an employer ever lied to you in a job interview?

Speaking activity

Ask a partner what they would do in the following situations:

- A shop assistant mistakenly gives you an extra $50 change. Do you keep it or tell the shop about the error?
- Your boss uses company money to pay for a weekend in Paris with his mistress. He asks you to lie and say it was a business trip. If you tell the truth, you risk being fired.
- Your girlfriend is on her way to a job interview and asks if you like her hair (you don't!). Do you lie or tell her the truth?

Partner Interview

- ❐ Have you ever been brutally honest and hurt someone's feelings? Tell the story.
- ❐ What would you do if someone spread lies about you?
- ❐ What kind of problems does dishonesty cause?
- ❐ How can you tell when someone is being dishonest? Body language? Eye contact?

Consolidation

Write down 3 statements about yourself, 2 of which are true and 1 of which is a lie. Students take turns reading out their 3 statements. After each student, other pupils write down which statement they think is a lie. The pupil with the statements should then reveal the truth. Award one point for a correct guess.

The pupil with the most points is the winner.

Hotels

Warm-up

How often do you stay at hotels? Did you enjoy the last hotel you stayed in? Why/why not? What was the best hotel you have ever stayed in? What made it so good?

Key Vocabulary

annoying / irritating / chain (of hotels) / luxury / to recommend / to give feedback / to check in / to check out / reception desk / porter / amenities / guest / room service / suite

Teacher → Pupil Questions

- ❐ Do you enjoy staying at hotels?
- ❐ Why do you normally stay at hotels? Conferences? Weddings? Business?
- ❐ What annoys you most about hotels?
- ❐ Have you ever stayed at a hotel that was part of the chain of hotels? Describe the experience.

Speaking activity

Discuss with a partner: What is most important to you when choosing a hotel? Consider:

- Facilities (gym, swimming pool, conference room, etc.)
- Location
- Price
- Level of luxury
- Service
- Food and restaurants

Report your partner's priorities to the class.

Partner Interview

- ❐ Which hotel chain do you recommend? Why?
- ❐ Have you ever stayed in a luxury hotel? Describe the experience.
- ❐ Compare a luxury hotel you have stayed in with a 'normal' hotel.
- ❐ Are luxury hotels worth the extra money?
- ❐ Describe your best/worst hotel experience. What made it so?

Consolidation

Did you enjoy your stay?

Design a simple questionnaire with which hotel guests can give feedback after their stay. Make statements that can be evaluated using a scale from 1 to 5. For example:
My room was kept clean and tidy at all times.

1 = I agree completely
2 = I agree
3 = I agree somewhat
4 = I disagree
5 = I disagree completely

Then ask a classmate to fill out your questionnaire for the last hotel they stayed in. Afterwards, ask them the reasons for their ratings.

Report your partner's responses to the class.

Individuality

Warm-up

Does your job give you the chance to be an individual? If so, how? If not, why not? Is it important to you to be different or to express yourself in a unique way?

Key Vocabulary

unique / to be original / to encourage someone / to conform / to fit in / to blend in / to stick out

Teacher → Pupil Questions

- Do you prefer to blend in or stick out? Why?
- In which kinds of jobs do you think individuality is valued?
- Do you like to wear the latest trends or do you prefer to be 'fashionably different?'
- Would you like more opportunities to be an individual?
- Which experience has been most important in making you the person you are today?

Speaking activity

Imagine you are at a party. Stand up, circulate and find out one thing about each partygoer (your classmates) that makes them different from everyone else in the class. What is unique about them?

Share what you found out with the class.

Partner Interview

- How do you feel around people who are different from you? Do you find it easier to deal with people if you know what to expect?
- John Lennon wrote: 'There's nothing you can do that can't be done, there's nothing you can sing that can't be sung.' Is it difficult to do something original these days?
- What can you do especially well that most other people cannot do? What skill/talent makes you an individual?
- Did your education encourage you to be an individual or did it teach you to conform?
- Should parents encourage their children to conform or to be individuals? Do people have an easier life if they fit in with society?

Consolidation

Class discussion: 'Companies don't want people who are individuals, they want people who fit in with their corporate identity.'

Do you agree or disagree? Think about your personal experiences. Take 3 minutes to write down your opinions before the discussion begins.

Innovation and Creativity

Warm-up

Do schools in your country encourage a spirit of innovation and creativity? What was your experience in the education system? Does your job require you to be creative? How?

Key Vocabulary

a spirit of innovation / research and development / to think outside the box / unique selling point

Teacher → Pupil Questions

- Would you describe yourself as a creative/innovative person?
- Do you think people are born with creative talent or can creativity be learned?
- Would working in research and development interest you? Why/why not?
- Does your country have a reputation for being creative and innovative? In which areas?
- What innovative products do you use every day? What advantages do they give you?

Speaking activity

With a partner, discuss which skills, qualities and characteristics you think someone that works in research and development should have.

Then make a mind map of as many adjectives as you can think of to describe such a person.

Partner Interview

- Are people in your profession encouraged to think outside the box?
- What does innovation mean in your company?
- Which companies depend on innovation? How? Is this a good business model?
- Do you find innovative companies to be more attractive employers? Why/why not?
- Do you think technology helps us to be innovative? How?

Consolidation

You work for the R & D department at Cutting Edge Inc. Your company has asked you and a colleague (a classmate) to come up with some innovations for *one* of the following products: (a) the coffee mug, (b) the umbrella, (c) sunglasses. Your company is always searching for a 'unique selling point.'

You often find the following strategies work well:

- Find a common problem with the current product and solve it
- Combine 2 products (e.g. a coffee mug with Internet access)

Intelligence

Warm-up

Do you think intelligent people are more successful, or doesn't intelligence play a role? Which intelligences are most needed in your profession? Which are not needed?

Key Vocabulary

to develop / experiences / competencies / abilities / to lack (intelligence) / genius

Teacher → Pupil Questions

- ❒ Who is the most intelligent person you know? What makes them so intelligent, in your opinion?
- ❒ Which type of intelligence would you like to develop?
- ❒ Do you think society values some intelligences more highly than others? Which ones?

Speaking activity

Howard Gardner's Theory of Multiple Intelligences identifies a number of intelligence 'types':

- Bodily-kinaesthetic (movement and coordination)
- Interpersonal (social)
- Verbal-linguistic (language and words)
- Logical-mathematical (logical reasoning)
- Intrapersonal (self-reflection)
- Visual-spatial
- Musical
- Naturalistic (relationship to your environment)

Which of these intelligence types do you think is your strongest intelligence? Which is your weakest? Put the list in order from strongest to weakest, and then tell a partner why you arranged them as you did. Ask your partner which intelligences were encouraged during their childhood and education. Which were not encouraged? Report to the class.

Partner Interview

- ❒ Have you ever taken an IQ test? Did the result match your expectations?
- ❒ Is intelligence is something you are born with, or does it depend on your experiences?
- ❒ 'Highly intelligent people sometimes lack social competencies.' Do you agree or disagree?

Consolidation

With a partner, design a short test for one of Gardner's intelligence types. Your test may take any form you wish: questions, responding to stimuli, reaction to a particular situation etc. Test one classmate, and then present both your test and the results to the class.

Internet

Warm-up

How much time do you spend on the Internet every week? Do you know anyone who spends too much time online? How much is 'too much' in your opinion? Do you think spending too much time in front of a computer affects your quality of life?

Key Vocabulary

eventually / to replace / to survive / ability / to regulate / competition / user generated content / to contribute

Teacher → Pupil Questions

- Which ways of communicating on the web do you use most?
- Do you think Internet news sites will eventually replace newspapers?
- How do you think newspapers should respond to competition from the net?
- Which other businesses do you think will not survive in the Internet-age?
- Do you know of any businesses that have already closed down because of Internet competition?

Speaking activity

Write a list of 5 websites you find useful or would recommend to a friend.

Swap lists with a partner. Explain to your partner why the 5 sites made it onto your list.

Partner Interview

- Would you ever download films or music from the Internet? Do you find this acceptable?
- Many musicians and filmmakers have lost their livelihoods to the Internet. Do you think illegal sharing should be regulated? Is this possible, in your opinion?
- Since Web 2.0, user generated content has become king. Do you contribute to blogs, wikis etc. online? Which platforms do you use?
- If you had a blog, what would you blog about?

Consolidation

Brainstorm with a partner: How do you think the Internet will change in future? What will we be able to do on the Internet in 20 years time that we cannot do now? What would you like to be able to do online that is not yet possible?

Share your ideas with the class.

Investing

Warm-up

Are you good at investing? What makes a good investor? Do you know anyone that is a successful investor? What are their skills and personal qualities?

Key Vocabulary

return on investment / wealth / value / shares / stocks / risk / asset

Teacher → Pupil Questions

- What kinds of companies do you like to invest in? Which industries look promising?
- Would you invest in the company that you work for?
- Do you think green investments are a good investment?
- What are the advantages of letting an investment manager invest for you?
- Which *locations* are good investments? Emerging markets? Politically stable markets?

Speaking activity

With a partner, create a list of dos and don'ts for beginner investors. Your aim is to help them learn about investing by giving them good principles without exposing them to a lot of risk.

Share your dos and don'ts with the class.

Partner Interview

- Do you prefer safer investments such as bonds and big corporations or riskier investments such as start-up companies? What are the advantages and disadvantages?
- If you were to give someone an investment tip for the future, what would it be?
- Peter Lynch once wrote: 'Always invest in a business any idiot could run, because pretty soon any idiot will be running it!' Do you agree?
- What are the pros and cons of stocks versus bonds?

Consolidation

You are a stockbroker and in 10 minutes you have a meeting with the new client. You want to recommend buying shares in _____ (insert company of your choice). Prepare a one-minute presentation for the client outlining the advantages (and possible risks) of investing in this company.

Present to the class.

Class discussion: Which presentation was most convincing? Whose stock would you buy?

Job Interviews

Warm-up

Are you good at job interviews? What tips would you give your son or daughter before they went to their first job interview?

Key Vocabulary

to apply (for a job) / member of staff / nervous / to master nerves / honest / face-to-face / career gap / strengths / weaknesses / responsibilities / qualifications / skills / salary

Teacher → Pupil Questions

- How do you find information about a company you have applied to before an interview?
- Do you think it is possible to find out what a company is *really* like before you work there?
- Would you ever call a company to find out about it by talking to a member of staff?
- Are there any interview questions that make you nervous?
- Are employers always 100% honest in interviews? Are *you* 100% honest in interviews?

Speaking activity

Do you get nervous during job interviews? Do you have any strategies for dealing with nerves?

With a partner, come up with 5 tips for mastering nerves in interview situations.

Share with the class.

Partner Interview

- Describe your best/worst interview. What made it so good/bad?
- Have you ever had an interview by videoconference? What are the pros and cons of this format?
- What differences are there between video interviews and face-to-face interviews?
- How would you prepare for a video interview? Would you prepare any differently?
- How would you handle the following questions. Can you explain the 3-year gap in your CV? Why did you leave your last job? What are your weaknesses?

Consolidation

Write a short advertisement for your dream job. Give a one-sentence description of the company/organisation and include a few bullet points about the following: (a) responsibilities, (b) qualifications needed and (c) skills needed.

Give your dream job advertisement to a classmate and let them interview you for your dream job.

Jobs

Warm-up

What do you do for a living? Which jobs have you done in the past? How do these jobs compare? Which did you enjoy the most? Which was the most exhausting? Which was the most interesting?

Key Vocabulary

profession / to earn a living / employed / self-employed / security / salary

Teacher → Pupil Questions

- What do you like about your current job?
- What would you change about your job if you had the chance?
- Do you do your job because it interests you or simply to earn a living?
- Which industries do you think are growing and creating jobs at the moment?

Speaking activity

What do you look for in a job? How important to you are the following aspects?

- Job security
- Salary
- Flexibility
- Friendly colleagues
- Good boss
- Nice company atmosphere?

Reorder the list above, starting with the most important. Explain your choices to the class.

Partner Interview

- Have you ever considered being self-employed? What are the advantages/disadvantages?
- Does your job form part of your identity?
- How much responsibility do you want in your job?
- Do you think it is better to be a manager or a 'normal' employee?

Consolidation

Which jobs will still exist 50 years in the future? Which jobs won't exist? Which completely new jobs or professions might be created in 50 years?

Take a few minutes to write down your ideas. Then discuss this topic with the class.

Job Search

Warm-up

Do you find it easy or difficult to find jobs that match your skills and interests? How did you get the jobs you have done in the past? Contacts? Speculative applications? What would be your ideal job?

Key Vocabulary

networking / business contacts / recruiter / application / speculative application / careers fair

Teacher → Pupil Questions

- How do you search for jobs? Internet? Newspaper? Recruiting services?
- What are the advantages of searching for a job on employment websites?
- Do you search for jobs in newspapers? Which newspaper do you find most helpful?
- Which job search platform/service would you recommend to a friend?

Speaking activity

Are you good at networking? Draw a mind map of the different networks (personal and professional) that might help you find a new job (e.g. friends, customers, et cetera).

Ask a partner: Which 3 people from your networks do you think would help you the most? Why do you think these particular people would be helpful contacts?

Partner Interview

- What are the advantages (if any) of using a professional recruiting company?
- Do you tailor your applications to individual jobs? Why is this important?
- Have you ever applied for a job even though you did not meet all the criteria?
- Do you send speculative applications? Have you had any success with this approach?

Consolidation: Role Play

Role A: You are a recruiter for a large pharmaceutical company. You are currently attending a careers fair and you are on the lookout for a new employee for your diagnostics department. This position has been vacant for six months and your company desperately needs someone to start as soon as possible. You have been authorised to offer a likely candidate any incentive that you think is appropriate. A professional looking woman is approaching you now. Greet her.

Role B: You have just graduated with a PhD in pharmacy. You specialise in diagnostics. You are an excellent student and already have a good job offer. This offer includes a company car, 40 days holiday a year and a generous bonus system. You are attending a careers fair on the off chance you find something better. You are approaching the PNP Diagnostics stand. Greet the recruiter.

Leadership Styles

Warm-up

Have you ever been in a leadership position? Do you enjoy leading? If not, would you like to be in a leadership position? What are the pros and cons of being a leader?

Key Vocabulary

autocratic / to delegate / soft skills / ability / to make decisions / to be decisive / responsibility / communication / to supervise / supervisor

Teacher → Pupil Questions

- ❒ Do you think some people are born with natural leadership ability?
- ❒ Is it possible to learn to be a good leader?
- ❒ Why is good leadership so important for a business?
- ❒ Are there differences between male and female leadership styles?
- ❒ Do you think some men have difficulty following a female leader? Why?

Speaking activity

There are many different leadership styles, from 'autocratic' to 'participative' (democratic).

With a partner, discuss which style you prefer. Does it depend on the situation or industry? How would you describe your boss's leadership style? What is your style?

Share your attitudes with the class.

Partner Interview

- ❒ If you were the leader of your company, what changes would you make?
- ❒ 'Good leadership filters down to everybody and creates a good atmosphere.' Do you agree?
- ❒ What are the characteristics of a good leader?
- ❒ What leadership qualities do you most admire?
- ❒ Have you ever had to work for someone with bad leadership skills?

Consolidation

Your CEO has asked you to write a list of guidelines for middle managers in your company. With a partner, create a list of dos and don'ts for employees in leadership positions.

Share your ideas with the class.

Marketing

Warm-up

With a partner, write your own definition of the word *Marketing*. What does marketing mean to you? Share your definition with another pair and discuss the differences. Share with the class.

Key Vocabulary

recommendations / to establish rapport / testimonial / social proof / to engage a customer

Teacher → Pupil Questions

- What products does your company sell? How are the products marketed?
- Would working in marketing interest you? Why/why not?
- What characteristics and skills do you think someone needs to work in marketing?
- Have you ever had to market yourself (e.g. for a job interview)? Is this easy or difficult?

Speaking activity

You work as a career guidance counsellor. You frequently counsel young people that say they would like to make a career in Marketing and Advertising. With a partner, create a questionnaire that is designed to find out if a person is suitable for this profession. Consider personal qualities, skills, interests and talents.

Survey your classmates and report to the class why they are/aren't suitable for this profession.

Partner Interview

- What is your favourite product? Is it marketed well? Why?
- Do you usually buy things based on your friends' recommendations?
- Which products strike you as having exceptionally good marketing? Why?
- What marketing strategies does your company use? Do you think they are effective?

Consolidation

You work for Only White Inc. Sales of your most popular product (a tooth-whitening kit) are down. Your boss has asked you and your team to re-do the sales page on the company website. Specifically, she has asked you to include the following:

- A catchy headline
- An opening paragraph that establishes rapport with the customer
- A transformational success story that engages the customer
- Social proof, in the form a testimonial

Allocate the jobs above to pairs. Put the sales page together at the end and share with the team.

Meetings

Warm-up

How often do you go to meetings and what type of meetings are they? Do you ever find attending meetings a waste of time?

Key Vocabulary

participant / participation / to contribute / contribution / to attend (a meeting) / warring parties / chairperson / productive / unproductive / agenda

Teacher → Pupil Questions

- How do you prepare for the meetings you attend?
- What factors make a productive meeting, in your opinion?
- Have you ever had to attend a meeting that was not relevant to you? What is the best way to make sure that only people who *need* to be there are at the meeting?
- Do you prefer meetings with no fixed structure or meetings with a clear agenda?

Speaking activity

'I make all the participants in my meetings stand up to have the meeting. Sometimes we go for a walk while we have our meetings. People don't get too comfortable. This stimulates creativity.'

Ask a classmate if these strategies would work in their company meetings. Why/why not?

Report you partner's responses to the class.

Partner Interview

- In your opinion, what is the best way to deal with (a) punctuality problems, (b) participants that contribute too much, (c) strong opinions, (d) lack of participation, (e) warring parties, (f) people using smartphones, tablets or laptops during the meeting.
- When is a meeting *not* the best format?
- Some people say a fixed agenda is not a good idea for brainstorming/creative meetings. Do you agree or disagree?
- What are the pros and cons of video conferencing compared to meeting in person?
- Do you have any strategies for making group decisions during meetings?

Consolidation

What qualities do you think a good chairperson needs? With a partner, make a list of what you think are the most important qualities.

Share with the class.

Memory

Warm-up

Have you ever forgotten something important, such as an anniversary or birthday? Are you better at remembering names or numbers? Why do you think this is?

Key Vocabulary

to be forgetful / to reminisce / anniversary / photographic memory / dementia / to loose your memory / to have a mind like a sieve / long term memory / short term memory

Teacher → Pupil Questions

- Is having a good memory an advantage in your profession?
- Would you describe yourself as a forgetful person or is your memory reliable?
- What things do you find easiest to remember? What do you find most difficult?
- Do you like to reminisce about the past? Why/why not?

Speaking activity

Do you have any strategies for remembering important things, such as names, numbers, dates and passwords? Describe your strategies to a partner.

Report your partner's strategies to the class.

Partner Interview

- If you had a photographic memory, how would your life change?
- Do you think people can be trained to have a better memory?
- Which is better, your long-term memory or your short-term memory?
- Describe one of your earliest memories.
- Sometimes music, places, sounds and smells can trigger memories. Has this ever happened to you? What was the memory?

Consolidation

You work for an architectural company and your department is responsible for interior design. You have recently been asked to design an old-people's home for patients with dementia. These patients are slowly loosing their memories and need an environment in which they can orientate themselves that makes their lives easier on a day-to-day basis.

Meet with 2 of your colleagues and brainstorm a few initial ideas for the project.

Present your ideas to the class.

Money

Warm-up

Are you good at saving? What do you do that makes you a good/bad saver? Are you saving for anything at the moment? What have you saved for in the past? How long did it take you?

Key Vocabulary

to spend / to pay for something / to donate / salary / bank account / obsolete / income / to invest / to earn money / bank loan / to borrow / interest rates

Teacher → Pupil Questions

- ❒ What are your spending habits?
- ❒ Do you prefer to pay by cash, card or phone? Why?
- ❒ Do you think paper money will still exist in 50 years? Will it eventually become obsolete?
- ❒ What are the advantages/disadvantages of paying in cash? What about paying by card?
- ❒ Do you worry about security when buying something online?
- ❒ What are the advantages/disadvantages of using PayPal instead of a credit card?

Speaking activity: Role Play

Role A: Your uncle has died and left you $300,000. You are not very good with money and need some advice on how to invest (or spend) the money. You have heard that interest rates are low at the moment and that simply leaving the money in the bank is not the most sensible option. You have a friend who is quite good with money. Give him/her a call and ask for advice.

Role B: You are quite good with money, having worked as a financial advisor for a few years. Friends often ask you for informal financial advice. Your phone is ringing. Answer it.

Partner Interview

- ❒ What are your saving habits?
- ❒ Have you ever donated money to a charity?
- ❒ Is there a large gap between rich and poor in your country? Is the gap getting smaller or is it widening?
- ❒ Do you think governments should regulate the financial system or give it more freedom?
- ❒ 'Money is the root of all evil.' Do you agree or disagree?

Consolidation

What would you do if you had a private income and didn't have to work for a living? Would your life change? If so, how?

Write down some ideas and present them to the class.

Motivation

Warm-up

What do you do to keep your motivation high during a difficult task? Have you ever tried to motivate someone else to do something? Were you successful? How did you feel afterwards?

Key Vocabulary

internal motivation / external motivation / to increase / prestige / successful

Teacher → Pupil Questions

- How are you best motivated?
- Have you ever had a motivating/un-motivating boss? What made them so?
- Who is the most motivating person you have ever met? Why?
- Were you a motivated pupil in school? Why/why not?

Speaking activity

With a partner, come up with a definition of 'motivation' in your own words. What does motivation mean to you?

Get together with another pair and share your definitions. Compare your definitions and combine the best elements of each to form a new, improved definition.

Share your definition with the class.

Partner Interview

- Do you have naturally high internal motivation or do you respond better to external motivation (e.g. bonuses or praise)? Give examples from you own experience.
- Do you find it motivating to be given responsibility for something?
- What is the best way to help people to increase their motivation?
- What do you find more motivating, prestige or money?

Consolidation

Your boss has asked you to write some guidelines for the team leaders in your company. Your recommendations should help team leaders to understand how very can energise and motivate their teams.

Consider the following: (a) communication, (b) praise, (c) rewards, and (d) responsibilities.

Report your recommendations to the class.

Movies

Warm-up

Who is your favourite actor? Why? What do you think was their best performance? Do you have a favourite director? What makes this director's films more interesting than other films?

Key Vocabulary

genre / performance / low-budget film / director / character / review / to recommend / illegal / plot / special effects

Teacher → Pupil Questions

- Do you prefer Hollywood blockbusters or low budget films?
- Where do you go to get film reviews and recommendations?
- How do you think films today compare with films from 20 years ago? What about films from 40 years ago?
- How do films from your country compare to Hollywood films?
- What do you think will be the most popular way to watch films in the future? Streaming services? Cinemas? TV?

Speaking activity

With a partner, brainstorm as many film genres as you can think of (thriller, romance, crime, et cetera).

Then put the list in order, starting with your favourite genre and ending with your *least* favourite.

Explain to a partner why you enjoy your first genre and don't enjoy your last genre.

Partner Interview

- Describe the best/worst movie you have ever seen. Why was it so good/bad?
- If someone made a movie of your life, whom would you like to play the lead role?
- Would you ever download a movie illegally? Do you think the Internet has damaged the film industry permanently?
- How do you think films will be different in the future?

Consolidation

Pupil A: Think of a film you have seen recently. Give your partner a 'verbal review' of the film, explaining why you recommend (or don't recommend) the film.

Pupil B: Listen to pupil A's film review. Then tell the class if you will watch this film or not after listening to your partner's review. What persuaded you or put you off watching the film?

Networking

Warm-up

Are you good at networking? What do you think makes a good networker? Do you enjoy networking or do you think of it as a necessary evil?

Key Vocabulary

to make a good impression / to have something in common / appropriate / sincere / trade fair

Teacher → Pupil Questions

- What are normally your main goals when networking?
- Which settings do you find most useful when networking? Trade fairs? Conferences?
- Describe the last trade fair you visited. Was it useful for networking? Who did you meet?
- Do you ever network by email? What are the pros and cons?
- 'Following up' after making a new contact is the most important part. Do you agree? What is the best way to follow up, in your opinion?

Speaking activity

Networking experts often say that the goal of networking should be to help other people. What do you think is meant by this? Do you agree or disagree with this idea?

Discuss with a partner and report your ideas to the class.

Partner Interview

- Do you have a business card? What are the advantages/disadvantages of using a business card? Do you think business cards will ever become obsolete?
- Do you ever find networking uncomfortable? If so, why?
- What is the best way not to appear pushy and insincere while networking?
- 'Networking is more about listening to others than saying the right things.' Do you agree?

Consolidation

Which of the following tips do you think is most important when networking?
- Smile
- Make eye contact
- Ask questions
- Practise frequently
- Dress comfortably

Prioritise the list. Then compare your list with a classmate's list. Explain the reasons for your choices.

News and Media

Warm-up

Where do you get your news (TV, app, radio, internet)? Which newspaper do you read and why? Which newspaper would you recommend to others?

Key Vocabulary

newspaper / tabloid / broadsheet / reliable / trustworthy / report / source / balanced / sensational / headline / TV station / TV channel

Teacher → Pupil Questions

- Which sections of the newspaper interest you most?
- Has technology changed the way you get your news?
- What is your favourite news programme?
- Which TV stations are a good source of news? Which are not a good source?
- What do you think of the quality of news reporting in your country?

Speaking activity

What are the advantages/disadvantages of reading news on the Internet? With a partner, make a list of the pros and cons.

Report your ideas to the class.

Partner Interview

- What is your opinion of sensational news reporting in tabloid newspapers?
- Do you trust the news you read on the Internet? What is the best way to make sure this news is reliable and trustworthy?
- How do public TV stations compare with private stations in your country?
- Is the Internet putting traditional newspapers out of business? What is the future for newspapers, in your opinion?
- How do you think we will consume news in the future?

Consolidation

Select 2 stories that you are following in the news at the moment. With a partner, try to come up with an eye-catching newspaper headline for each story. Your goal is to get the reader to continue reading.

Share with the class.

The class should vote on the best headline and explain the reasons for their choice.

Nuclear Power

Warm-up

Is your country dependent on energy that is imported from other countries? Could nuclear energy be the answer? What alternatives are there to nuclear power?

Key Vocabulary

power plant / toxic / renewable energy / to be dependent on / to trust / to maintain / inevitable / to take precautions / carbon dioxide

Teacher → Pupil Questions

- ❐ Would you be willing to pay more for energy if it came from renewable sources?
- ❐ Do you trust some countries to maintain nuclear power stations but not others?
- ❐ Do you think we should accept nuclear accidents as inevitable?
- ❐ What precautions should we take for the possibility of another nuclear accident?
- ❐ Are you for or against nuclear power? Why?

Speaking activity

Which of the following would you rather live next to?

- A nuclear-power plant
- A chemical company that made toxic chemicals
- An area where fracking was being used to extract oil?

Discuss briefly with a partner and report your reasons to the class.

Partner Interview

- ❐ What are the biggest pros and cons of nuclear energy?
- ❐ Which issue do you think will be more problematic in the future: nuclear waste or the melting of the polar ice caps? Why?
- ❐ Nuclear power creates the most energy with the least amount of carbon dioxide. What do you think is the best alternative to nuclear power?
- ❐ Renewable energy is more expensive and more difficult to produce in larger quantities. Is nuclear energy the answer to providing energy to poorer third and second world countries?

Consolidation

Search for 'facts about nuclear power' on the Internet. Read for 5 minutes.

Report any facts you found surprising to the class and discuss.

Occasions

Warm-up

What was the last occasion you celebrated? How did you celebrate? What do you enjoy more, being a host, or being a guest? Why?

Key Vocabulary

to celebrate / celebration / to invite / invitation / host / guest / special occasion

Teacher → Pupil Questions

- Do you prefer to go to formal occasions or informal occasions?
- Describe the best party you have ever been to. What made it special?
- Describe the worst party you have ever been to. What went wrong?
- Are there any occasions that are important in your country but not in other countries?

Speaking activity

Imagine you are at a party. Stand up, circulate and find out which special occasions the other partygoers (your classmates) enjoy the most. Which do they enjoy the least?

Did you notice any trends or common preferences? Share them with the class.

Partner Interview

- Do you celebrate different occasions with different people? Which occasions do you celebrate with friends, with family, or with colleagues?
- Are you married? How did you celebrate your wedding?
- Are you single? If you had a wedding, how would you like to celebrate it?
- What are the pros and cons of big weddings versus small weddings?
- 'Marriage has lost its meaning in the 21st-century.' Do you agree or disagree?

Consolidation

If you could invite anyone in the world (living or dead) to your birthday party, which 3 people would you invite and why?

Share your list with the class and explain why you find the 3 people on your list interesting.

Parenting

Warm-up

What is the nicest thing about having children? What is the most difficult thing about being a parent? What makes a good parent, in your opinion?

Key Vocabulary

to raise children / to take care of children / values / vaccination / to pass something on / similar / different / to be under pressure

Teacher → Pupil Questions

- Which age group is most difficult to parent, in your opinion?
- What values would you like to pass on to your children?
- Do you think it is important to 'push' children to be successful in school?
- If you have more than one child, how are your children similar and how are they different?
- If you could start over as a parent, would you do anything differently?

Speaking activity

'Before I got married I had six theories about raising children; now, I have six children and no theories.' (John Wilmot)

Ask a partner if they have (or had!) any theories about raising children.

Report their responses to the class.

Partner Interview

- Are you for or against the vaccination of children? What are the advantages and disadvantages?
- Did you do things differently with your second child than you did with your first child?
- 'Today women have to have a perfect career, be a perfect mother and be a perfect homemaker.' Do you think women are under too much pressure?
- Do you think men are under similar pressure? If not, what pressures do you think men experience as a result of becoming parents?

Consolidation

Ask a partner to compare their life *before* they became a parent with their life *after* they became a parent.

Report the similarities and differences between your experiences to the class.

Performance Reviews and Feedback

Warm-up

Do you find performance reviews helpful? What is the purpose of a performance review in your company? How is good performance encouraged in your company?

Key Vocabulary

rewards / to encourage / to evaluate / praise / criticism / to supervise / targets / goals

Teacher → Pupil Questions

- What makes a useful performance review?
- Have you ever had to evaluate your own performance?
- Have you ever had to evaluate someone else's performance?
- What is the best way to give feedback in such a situation?
- How many people is it possible for a boss to supervise effectively?

Speaking activity

Do you think that performance should be linked to bonuses and rewards? With a partner, list the advantages and disadvantages of this system.

Share your ideas with the class.

Partner Interview

- Do you think it is important to balance praise and criticism when giving feedback? Is this different in other cultures?
- Should school pupils be able to evaluate their teachers' performance? Why/why not?
- What goals did you agree on at your last performance review? Did you meet the targets from the previous review?
- Do you ever give your boss feedback? Do you find this task easy or difficult?
- Do you think subordinates should be allowed to evaluate their superior's performance?

Consolidation

Employees mostly get feedback from their boss. In some companies, employees get feedback from other sources as well, e.g. customers, colleagues, and team members. Would this idea work at your company?

With a partner, write down the pros and cons of this idea.

Share with the class and explain why this idea would work/would not work at your company.

Personality

Warm-up

Do you think your job suits your personality? How? How important is it to have a job that suits your personality? Which character traits do you look for in (a) a partner, (b) a friend, (c) a colleague?

Key Vocabulary

characteristics / character traits / introvert / extrovert / opposites attract / quiet / curious / shy / patient / impatient / sensitive / honest / dishonest / talkative / chatty / good sense of humour

Teacher → Pupil Questions

- What are your personality traits?
- Do you think you are an introvert or an extrovert?
- Do you think personality traits can be passed on from parents or other family members?
- Do you like people with strong or dominant personalities?
- What types of personality do you find attractive?

Speaking activity

With a partner, discuss which characteristics you like to see in a boss/manager. Which characteristics don't you like? What experiences have you had with bosses in the past?

Make a list of (a) positive characteristics a boss *should* have and (b) negative characteristics a boss *shouldn't* have.

Share with the class.

Partner Interview

- What experiences have shaped your personality the most?
- Is it 'better' to be an extrovert? Are introverts more intelligent? Is there any truth in these stereotypes?
- 'Opposites attract.' Do you agree or disagree?
- Is there anything about your personality that you would like to change?
- Describe the personalities in your family.
- If you had a split personality, which character would you like to have as your alter ego?

Consolidation

With a partner, create a short 'Personality Test' to find out which of your classmates are introverts and which are extroverts. You test should contain 5 questions. E.g. 'Do you find parties exhausting or energising?' Test your classmates and share the results with the class.

Privacy and Data Protection

Warm-up

Does your company take data protection seriously? How do they make sure data is safe?

Key Vocabulary

data protection / surveillance / to invade (someone's privacy) / a threat (to privacy) / to monitor / secrets / to leak information

Teacher → Pupil Questions

- Do you feel safe in public places? Do surveillance cameras in public make you feel safer?
- Are you careful about what information you give out on the web?
- Do you feel that social networking sites are a threat to your privacy?
- Do you think governments should be allowed to invade people's privacy in the interests of national security? How would you feel if a government employee read your email?

Speaking activity

With a partner, discuss the data protection measures at companies/organisations you have worked for in the past. Then create a 5-point plan for companies that want to improve their data protection measures.

Share with the class.

Partner Interview

- Do you feel you have more privacy in your country than in other countries or less privacy? Why?
- How careful are you with: (a) your email address, (b) your phone number, (c) your name and address, (d) your customer's personal data, (e) your banking information?
- 'You only need privacy if you are involved in illegal activities.' Do you agree or disagree?
- Do you think sites like Wikileaks are a good thing or a bad thing?

Consolidation

In your opinion, which of the following are the biggest threat to privacy?

- Employers monitoring employee use of the Internet during working hours
- CCTV cameras in streets and shops
- Search engines keeping track of your search terms
- Governments spying on individuals in the interest of national security

With a partner, put the list in order starting with what you think is the biggest threat to privacy.

Report your reasons to the class.

Productivity

Warm-up

What is your most productive time of the day? Why? Does the company you work for have any strategies for increasing productivity?

Key Vocabulary

distraction / to be thrown off track / efficient / effective / open-plan office / deadline

Teacher → Pupil Questions

- Do you find it difficult to avoid distractions at work?
- What do you find most distracting? Emails? Meetings? Phone calls? Talkative colleagues?
- Describe you energy levels throughout a typical day.
- Many people arrive at work early to get things done before their colleagues arrive. Are you one of these people? What are the drawbacks of this strategy?
- Have you ever worked in an open-plan office? What are the advantages/disadvantages?

Speaking activity

With a partner, come up with your own definition of the word *productivity*.

Compare your definition with another group's definition. Discuss and adjust your definitions to come up with a 'definitive' final definition.

Share with the class

Partner Interview

- Do you think technology (apps, computer programs etc.) can help you to be productive?
- What is the best way to stop distractions affecting your productivity (talkative colleagues, answering emails, incoming phone calls)?
- What is the best way to stop social media and the Internet from affecting your productivity?
- Do you find you work better under pressure? Are deadlines useful for productivity?

Consolidation

You have been asked by your boss to meet with 2 of your colleagues (classmates) to create a list of recommendations and suggestions for improving productivity in your company. Your boss would like to hear a range of suggestions for all types of employee from sales to administrators across the company.

Present your recommendations to the class.

Qualifications

Warm-up

What are your qualifications? Are there any qualifications you would like to have but don't? Which qualifications do you think are most useful to have?

Key Vocabulary

employer / employee / training / certificate / apprenticeship / degree / masters / doctorate (PhD) / post-doctorate

Teacher → Pupil Questions

- Which qualifications would you advise your children to pursue? Why?
- Which jobs can you do without any qualifications? Do you know of any successful people who do not have any qualifications?
- Do you find your training and qualifications useful in your daily work?
- Did you get any careers advice when you were in school? What were you advised? Do you think it was good advice?

Speaking activity

What is your dream job? Describe your dream job to a partner and have your partner describe their dream job to you.

Ask you partner what qualifications would be necessary to get their dream job.

Partner Interview

- Have you ever gotten a qualification that was a waste of time or not relevant to your future career?
- What are the minimum qualifications needed to do your job?
- Which do you think is more important, qualifications or experience?
- Do you think the parents should have to do a parenting qualification before they become parents?
- Do you think that politicians should have to be qualified before they become politicians?

Consolidation

Discuss briefly with a partner: If you were an employer, would you employ someone based on their qualifications, skills, character or another factor? Write a short list of what you think is important, starting with what you think is the *most* important factor.

Report your ideas to the class.

Relationships

Warm-up

Where and how did you meet your partner? Is it difficult to find a partner in your city/town? Are there lots of singles?

Key Vocabulary

attractive / sense of humour / to have something in common / personality / characteristics / to get on well with someone / to get along with someone / to get to know someone

Teacher → Pupil Questions

- Do women want different things from a relationship than men? What are the differences between men and women when it comes to relationships?
- What do you look for in a partner?
- Do you believe in love at first sight?
- If you are single, where is the best place to meet a new partner?

Speaking activity

Which of the following do you consider most important in a partner?

- Wealth (has lots of money)
- Has lots in common with you
- Is physically attractive
- Has a high status in society (job, well-known in their field, etc.)
- Has the same level of education as you do

Explain your choices to a partner. Report your partner's preferences to the class.

Partner Interview

- If you were single, would you ever consider using an Internet dating site?
- What do you think is the secret to a successful long-term relationship?
- What do you think are the pros and cons of getting married?
- Do you think there is a difference between 'love' and being 'in love?'
- 'Weekend relationships last longest. Banal, every-day life kills romance!' Do you agree?

Consolidation

The question 'What do women want?' has baffled psychologists for centuries! Get into small groups. Men should work only with other men, women with other women. Write a short list of bullet points describing what *you* think women want.

Read out each group's list and discuss the differences.

Remedies

Warm-up

How often do you come down with an illness or cold? Do you have a good immune system? Do you know any home remedies? What are they good for? Vitamin C is often said to help with colds and flu. What is your opinion?

Key Vocabulary

symptoms / ache / sick / ill / immune system / sore throat / cough / flu / a cold / fever / to take medicine / home remedy / to get sick / to get better / prescription / pharmacy / painkiller / antibiotics

Teacher → Pupil Questions

- When was the last time you got sick?
- What were your symptoms? How did you feel?
- Did you stay at home or go to work? Did you go to the doctor?
- Did the doctor give you a prescription?
- What advice did the doctor give you? How long did it take you to get better?

Speaking activity

Do you prefer alternative (natural) medicine or 'normal' medicine? Does it depend on the situation? With a partner, make a list of pros and cons for each.

Share with the class.

Partner Interview

- What would you recommend for (a) a cold, (b) the flu, (c) a sore throat, (d) a cough, (e) a fever, (f) a backache, (g) a headache, (h) a stomach-ache.
- Which painkiller do you prefer: aspirin, paracetamol or ibuprofen? What are the pros and cons?
- Which painkiller is best for children?
- When do you ask a pharmacist for advice and when do you ask a doctor? What are the pros and cons of going to a pharmacist as opposed to a doctor?

Consolidation: Role Play

Role A: You are not feeling so well. Explain your symptoms to your pharmacist and ask for advice.

Role B: You are a pharmacist. A customer that looks a little ill is coming into your pharmacy. Ask if you can help or if you can give him/her any advice.

Responsibility

Warm-up

What are your responsibilities at work? What is your *ideal* level of responsibility at work? Do you enjoy having lots of responsibility?

Key Vocabulary

to delegate / to volunteer / to accept responsibility / to take responsibility / to shirk responsibility / to avoid responsibility

Teacher → Pupil Questions

- Is it important for a boss/employer to trust employees and delegate responsibility?
- What are your responsibilities at home?
- Are you a parent? If so, have you become more responsible since becoming a parent?
- Do you think pay levels should be linked to responsibility?

Speaking activity

What are the advantages of having lots of responsibilities at work? What are the disadvantages? With a partner, create a list of the pros and cons.

Share your list with the class.

Partner Interview

- Are you someone who accepts responsibility or avoids responsibility? Does it depend on the situation?
- Should people in 'responsible' professions (surgeons, airline pilots etc.) have to take a 'responsibility test?'
- Do you think prospective parents should have to take a responsibility test?
- What should be the consequences for powerful people that abuse their responsibility?
- How responsible is the 'man in the street' for the environment in which he or she lives?

Consolidation

Design a survey of 5 questions to discover how responsible your classmates are. Then survey your classmates to find out who is the *most* responsible person in the class.

E.g. If your boss asked for a member of your department to lead a new project, would you volunteer?

Share your findings with the class and say how you came to those conclusions.

Restaurants

Warm-up

Ask a partner: Which of the following is most important to you when choosing a restaurant?

- Good service
- Pleasant atmosphere
- Value for money
- Excellent food
- Good wine list

Report your partner's responses to the class.

Key Vocabulary

value for money / crowded / delicious / superb / cosy / charming / lively / atmosphere / ambiance / bill / tip / service charge / cuisine / variety

Teacher → Pupil Questions

- ❒ Do you have a favourite restaurant? What makes it so good?
- ❒ What kind of ambience do you prefer in a restaurant? Relaxed? Lively? Romantic?
- ❒ Do you like a lot of variety in the restaurants you visit, or do you stick to what you know?
- ❒ What is the tipping culture like in your country? How does it compare to other countries?

Speaking activity

If you opened your own restaurant, which kind of restaurant would it be and why? Think about the (a) kind of food, (b) the décor, (c) the atmosphere and (d) the location.

Take a few minutes to write down a few key points and then share your ideas with the class.

Partner Interview

- ❒ Have you ever complained at a restaurant? What was the problem?
- ❒ Do you like to go to foreign restaurants? Which did you like the most/least?
- ❒ Is it easy to find restaurants that serve healthy foods in your city or area?
- ❒ Do you eat at fast food restaurants? Do you like the atmosphere at fast food restaurants?

Consolidation

Ask a partner to compare 2 restaurants to which they enjoy going.

Then tell your partner about your taste in restaurants and ask which of the 2 restaurants they would recommend.

Routines

Warm-up

Do you think it's important to have a routine? Why/why not? What are the advantages of having a clear routine?

Key Vocabulary

always / frequently / usually / often / sometimes / rarely / seldom / never / survey (n.) / predictable / spontaneous

Teacher → Pupil Questions

- What do you do a) every week, b) every weekend, c) every month, d) every year?
- What are a few things you usually do in summer? What do you never do?
- Name a few things you always do in winter. What do you rarely do in winter?
- What do you often do on the weekends? What do you seldom do?
- What tasks do you sometimes have to do at work? What do you frequently do at work?
- Do you normally fly first class, business class or economy class?

Speaking activity

Ask a partner to describe their daily routine.

Report your partner's routine to the class.

Partner Interview

- Does your routine stop you becoming stressed?
- Does having a routine make you more productive?
- 'Routines lead to a boring life without any spontaneity.' Do you agree?
- Some people have been known to go on holiday to the same place every year. Do you understand these people or do you find the idea boring?

Consolidation

Write a survey of 5 questions to discover who in your class is the most spontaneous and who is the most predictable.

Stand up, circulate and survey to your classmates.

Present your results to the class, explaining why pupil A is the most spontaneous, and pupil B the most predictable.

Sales

Warm-up

Do you think you would make a good salesperson? Why/why not? Would you ever consider going into Sales? Do you think salespeople have a good lifestyle?

Key Vocabulary

to convince / to persuade / campaign / values / attitude / sales pitch / sales targets / to negotiate

Teacher → Pupil Questions

- Do you have to be an extrovert to work in sales?
- What is your favourite product and what strategies are used to sell it?
- What sales strategies does your company use?
- Have you noticed any companies that have a very aggressive sales strategy? How do you react to this as a customer?

Speaking activity

What characteristics do you think are needed to be a good sales-person? With a partner, make a list of the personal qualities you think are necessary.

Share your results with the class.

Partner Interview

- If you were in sales, would you be willing to sell poor quality products?
- Ron Willingham wrote that 'selling is 85% attitude, values and emotional control.' Do you agree?
- Describe a sales campaign you find particularly good. Why does it work so well?
- Do you think traditional advertising has become less effective because we are constantly exposed to it?
- Sales people often get a bonus for reaching their sales targets. Do you think this is a good system?

Consolidation

Choose a product you would recommend to a friend and create a 30-second sales pitch for that product.

Present your sales pitch to a partner.

Evaluate your partner's sales pitch and report to the class if you found the pitch convincing.

School and Education

Warm-up

Do you think you received a good education? Do you think school education prepares people well for the job market? Did you feel well prepared?

Key Vocabulary

kindergarten / primary school / elementary school / secondary school / high school / college / university

Teacher → Pupil Questions

- ❒ Which subjects did you find most interesting at school? Which didn't you enjoy?
- ❒ Which is better: A general education in which pupils study *lots* of subjects or specialist education with only *a few* subjects?
- ❒ Did your country do well in the Pisa study? What is your opinion of such studies?
- ❒ When does the school day start and end in your country? How does this compare to other countries?

Speaking activity

Ask a partner to describe their path through the education system. What were the positives and negatives?

Report your partner's responses to the class.

Partner Interview

- ❒ Do you think pupils should be grouped according to academic ability or all taught together in one class?
- ❒ Girls mature faster than boys. Does this cause any issues or problems?
- ❒ Is there an argument for single sex schools?
- ❒ Do grind-schools give wealthier pupils an unfair advantage, in your opinion?
- ❒ What is your opinion of alternative education methods (Montessori/Waldorf/Steiner, et cetera)? Would you send your child to such a school?

Consolidation

'Private schools should be forbidden because they are better and give wealthier pupils an unfair advantage in life.'

Write 3 arguments *for* or *against* this statement.

Present your arguments and discuss with the class.

Senses

Warm-up

What is your favourite colour? What emotions do you associate with it? Do you associate other colours with other emotions? E.g. lavender is often considered restful, red associated with anger, etc.

Key Vocabulary

smell / touch / taste / sight / hearing / scenery / sweet / salty / bitter / sour / spicy / rough / smooth / fragrant / stinking / to associate (a smell with a particular memory)

Teacher → Pupil Questions

- What is your favourite flavour – sweet, salty, bitter, sour or spicy?
- Which flavours did you hate when you were younger that you now like?
- Which sense is most important for your job?
- What is your favourite smell?
- Can you work while listening to music/hearing noise in the background or do you need silence?

Speaking activity

Do you associate any smells with particular memories?

Describe such a memory to a partner and say why you think this smell triggers this memory.

Partner Interview

- What gives you the most pleasure: beautiful music, a delicious taste, beautiful scenery, the smell of chocolate, or the touch of a silk scarf?
- Which do you think is our most important sense?
- If you had to lose one sense, which would it be?
- Describe the most beautiful view, person or sight you have ever seen.
- What is your opinion of perfume? Do you love it or hate it? Does it depend on who is wearing it?
- What music do you enjoy listening to? What music don't you enjoy? Why?

Consolidation

Describe a memorable concert or event you attended to a partner. Focus on:

- The sights and colours that you saw
- The sounds/music you heard
- The taste of things you ate and drank
- The smells you experienced

Shopping

Warm-up

What is your favourite shop and why? What do you like/dislike about shopping? What do you enjoy shopping for? What things *don't* you like shopping for? Why?

Key Vocabulary

to shop around / to try something on / to bargain / to haggle / to compare prices / good quality / bad quality / shopping habits / sale / bargain / cheap / expensive / discount

Teacher → Pupil Questions

- Do you prefer large department stores or smaller shops? What are the pros and cons?
- Do you think men have a different attitude to shopping than women? In what ways?
- If you could buy anything you wanted, what would you buy first?
- Do you like shopping on the Internet?

Speaking activity

With a partner, list the advantages and disadvantages of shopping online as opposed to traditional store shopping. Discuss which you prefer for which products.

Share with the class.

Partner Interview

- With whom do you like to shop?
- Do you 'shop around' and go to lots of shops to compare prices before buying?
- When you buy something, what is most important to you: price, quality or fashion?
- Do you like to try clothes on before buying them?
- Are you good at bargaining with sales assistants? Is it common to haggle with sales assistants in your country?

Consolidation

What are your shopping habits? Circulate and find out about your classmates' shopping habits: Which shops do they prefer? Where do they do most of their shopping? Where do they shop for clothes? What about electrical goods?

Find out with whom you have the most in common. Whose shopping habits are closest to your own?

Afterwards, report to the class and say how your shopping habits are similar.

Small Talk

Warm-up

Do you know anyone who is good at making small talk? What makes them so good at it? Do you find it easy to make small talk? Can you always think of something to say?

Key Vocabulary

chatty / introvert / extrovert / a necessary evil / sociable / unsociable / appropriate / inappropriate / to regret / acquaintance / habits / preferences / background

Teacher → Pupil Questions

- Are you a very chatty person or do you prefer to let others do the talking?
- Do you enjoy small talk or do you think it is a 'necessary evil?'
- What are your favourite small talk topics? Which topics do you hate?
- Which topics are appropriate for small talk? Which topics are inappropriate or taboo?
- Do you think someone can learn to be good at small talk?

Speaking activity

Talk to a partner and try to discover 3 things that you have in common.

Report to the class (a) what you have in common and (b) how you found the experience; do you think this is a good approach to small talk?

Partner Interview

- Do you think you are an introvert or an extrovert? Is it better to be one or the other?
- Do you enjoy socialising with colleagues/customers or do you prefer to keep business and pleasure separate?
- Do long silences make you feel uncomfortable? Why/why not?
- Have you ever said something you regretted in a social situation? Tell the story.

Consolidation: Role Play

You are about to have a business lunch with a customer/acquaintance that you have met 3 times. The last 3 times was in a business context and you did not have a chance to ask them about themselves or to get to know them properly. This time, however, you will be alone with the client in a restaurant and there will be plenty of time for small talk.

Ask the customer about their: (a) eating habits and preferences, (b) family and friends, (c) background and education.

Smoking

Warm-up

Do you smoke? Why/why not? How old were you when you started and how did you start? Do people obey no-smoking laws in your country? Is there much social pressure to do this?

Key Vocabulary

passive smoking / cancer / to ban (smoking) / laws / health / harmful / to sue (somebody)

Teacher → Pupil Questions

- We hear a lot about the disadvantages of smoking, but what are the advantages?
- Do you know anyone who has quit smoking? How did they do it?
- How do you react if someone is smoking around you?
- If you are a smoker, has anyone ever asked you to stop smoking? What was your reaction?
- In some countries, smoking is banned in public places. Is this a fair, in your opinion?

Speaking activity

Some people think smoking should be banned in public places. Others feel this is going too far.

With a partner, create a 5-point plan for how smokers and non-smokers can co-exist.

Share your plan with the class.

Partner Interview

- In your opinion, should smokers pay more for health insurance?
- Smoking during pregnancy can be harmful not only to the mother, but also to the baby. Should it be illegal for pregnant women to smoke?
- In your opinion, should tobacco companies be held responsible for lung cancer cases?
- In the US, tobacco companies have been sued for selling harmful products. Do you think this could happen in your country?

Consolidation

You have recently been elected Minister for Health and you have promised to reduce smoking related illness in your country by 25 per cent. In a few minutes you have a meeting with a colleague to plan how you will achieve this. Some ideas include launching a public health campaign, banning smoking in public and increasing the tax on cigarettes by 500%.

Discuss the issue with your colleague (classmate) and present your ideas to the class.

Social Networking

Warm-up

Do you enjoy social networking, or do you dislike it? Why? Which social networks do you use? How does social networking compare with traditional networking?

Key Vocabulary

privacy / data protection / features / risks / benefits / advertising / to ban

Teacher → Pupil Questions

- What kind of personal information do you put on your profile page? How much are you comfortable sharing with the public?
- Do you think social networking sites ever use personal information for other purposes?
- Can you compare social networking platforms? What are their strengths and weaknesses?
- Which is the best social network, in your opinion? Which is the worst? Why?
- What are the best features of the social networks you use?
- Do you ever use social networks for business? How can social networking benefit businesses?

Speaking activity

Which features would you like to have on social networks that don't yet exist? With a partner, come up with 3 new features (or features you would like to see integrated) that you think would benefit users.

Share your ideas with the class.

Partner Interview

- What are the risks associated with using social networks?
- Do you find social networks a distraction from work? Do you think social networking should be banned in the workplace?
- Do you regard your social network contacts as 'friends' or 'acquaintances?'
- How do you feel about social networks being monetised through advertising, et cetera?
- Do you in stay in contact with old friends through social networking? Would you have lost contact if you hadn't had the opportunity to use social networks?

Consolidation

How would you feel about your children using social networks? With a partner, create a short list of guidelines for parents to help them keep their children safe when using social networks.

Share your guidelines with the class.

Sports

Warm-up

Which sports do you do? Which sports do you like to watch? Which professional sports-person do you admire the most?

Key Vocabulary

tedious / to admire someone / competitive / commitment / drive (n.) / ambitious

Teacher → Pupil Questions

- Do you prefer team sports or individual sports?
- Are there any sports you find tedious and boring?
- Do men watch too much football, in your opinion?
- Do you think professional sports people are paid too much in some sports? What do you think would be fair payment?

Speaking activity

Discuss briefly with a partner: Which personality traits and characteristics do you think someone needs to have to be a professional sports-person?

Make a short list and share with the class.

Partner Interview

- 'Professional sport is all about money.' Do you agree or disagree?
- Do you think there is a culture of doping in some sports? What do you think should be done about this?
- Have you ever tried an extreme sport? If not, would you like to?
- Which sports do you consider too dangerous?

Consolidation

You are thinking of taking up a new sport. Ask a partner which sport they practice and if they would recommend it for you. Ask about the (a) fitness level, (b) equipment, (c) costs, (d) risks and (e) commitment needed to do this sport.

Share your partner's responses with the class.

Stress

Warm-up

Which aspects of your work do you find stressful? Which situations make you feel stressed?

Key Vocabulary

workload / to be under pressure / calm / tense / anxious / to worry / to delegate / to prioritise / to pace yourself / stress level / relaxed / overwhelmed / to relieve stress / to cope / workload

Teacher → Pupil Questions

- Do you work to live or live to work?
- How do you make sure you have a good work-life balance?
- Which symptoms do you experience when you are stressed? Headache? Tension?
- What do you usually do to relieve stress?
- Do you find exercise, family time and social activities a good way to counter stress?

Speaking activity

"Every year my company expects me to do *more* work in *less* time. The world of work was much less stressful 20 years ago!"

How does your workload today compare with your workload a few years ago? Compare your experiences with a classmate's experiences.

Report any similarities or differences to the class.

Partner Interview

- Do you know anyone that deals with stress in a very positive way? Do you know anyone who deals with it in a negative way? Describe.
- Do you think a certain amount of stress can be a good thing in some situations?
- Would you find a stress-free life boring? Why/why not?
- Does technology help you to be less stressed or does it create more stress? How?

Consolidation

The employees in your company are stressed! Last year, 4 of your colleagues had to take time off because they were burnt out. Come up with a list of recommendations for reducing employee stress in your company. Your boss has one condition, however: productivity must remain the same.

With a classmate, create a list of recommendations to help employees. Share with the class.

Success

Warm-up

Who is the most successful person you know personally? Can you describe their personality? What makes them so successful in your opinion?

Key Vocabulary

to be ambitious / ambition / luck / to be successful / experience / influence / to dress for success

Teacher → Pupil Questions

- How important is success to you?
- Are you a very ambitious person?
- Do you think it's important to 'dress for success?'
- Do you think being successful makes people happy?
- Do you think is it possible to teach the people to be successful?

Speaking activity

Do you have a formula for success? With a partner, come up with your own 'formula for professional success.' Share with the class.

Which formula did you think was the best? Tell the class why.

Partner Interview

- Success means different things to different people. For some success means fame and money, for others it means family and community. What does success mean to you personally?
- Do you think success leads to more success?
- What is the best way to measure success?
- What has the biggest influence on success? Luck? Talent? Experience? Hard work?

Consolidation: Role Play

Role A: You are a successful pop psychologist and you are about to be interviewed by a chat show host. Topic: 'The Key to Success.' Write a few notes for yourself before you are interviewed.

Role B: You are a chat show host. Your ratings are down and you have been told that your chat show will be discontinued unless ratings improve. You are about to interview a successful pop psychologist on the topic: 'The Key to Success.' Write down a few questions you want to ask before you start the interview.

Superstitions

Warm-up

Are you a superstitious person? What are you superstitious about? Do you find superstitions childish? Were you superstitious when you were a child? Do you think people were more superstitious in the past?

Key Vocabulary

irrational / good luck / bad luck / strange / touch wood / mascot / myth / folklore

Teacher → Pupil Questions

- Do you know anyone who is superstitious? In what way are they superstitious?
- Have you ever avoided doing something because of a superstition? What was it?
- Have you ever blown out candles on a birthday cake and made a wish? Have you ever thrown a coin into a fountain and made a wish? Do you think of yourself as superstitious?
- Do you wear anything to bring you luck?

Speaking activity

In English speaking countries walking under a ladder is thought to be unlucky. Ask a classmate what is considered unlucky in their culture.

Together, try to come up with a possible explanation for how this superstition might have originated.

Share with the class.

Partner Interview

- Describe a time when you were exceptionally lucky. What happened?
- Describe a time when you were exceptionally *un*lucky. What happened?
- Do you have a lucky number?
- Are any particular numbers considered lucky in your culture?
- Do you play team sports or are you a sports fan? If so, does your team have a mascot for luck?

Consolidation

Are there any myths in your culture that contain superstitions? In 3 minutes, write down a few keywords to help you put the story together.

Then tell the story to a partner. If you come from the same culture as your classmates, choose a myth you both know and discuss it to help you remember it before telling the class.

Technology

Warm-up

Do you enjoy hearing about the latest technologies? Are you good with technology? Do you always buy the latest gadgets?

Key Vocabulary

gadget / invention / inventor / innovation / creativity / cutting-edge / technological advances

Teacher → Pupil Questions

- What is your favourite piece of technology? Why?
- What is the most innovative piece of technology you have heard about recently?
- Does technology make you more productive or less productive? How?
- What do you think will be the biggest technological change in the next few years?

Speaking activity

Discuss with a partner: How will technology change our lives in the next 50 years? Which technology will bring the biggest changes?

Report your ideas to the class.

Partner Interview

- What have been the main technological advances during your lifetime?
- Which technologies do you use everyday? Which do you never use? Why?
- In your opinion, what is the most important piece of technology ever invented?
- Do you think we are too dependent on technology?
- Which technologies do you think will become dominant when oil finally runs out?

Consolidation

Prioritise the technologies below, starting with the technology you think is the *most* important. Give reasons for your choices.

- Refrigeration
- Electricity
- The Internet
- GPS
- The 3D Printer.

Compare your list with a classmate's list and try to agree on the final order.

Television

Warm-up

What kinds of programmes do you generally watch on television? What is your favourite programme? Is there a good selection of TV programmes in your country? Do you like to watch reality TV?

Key Vocabulary

TV channel / TV station / TV program / advertising / advertisements (ads) / selection / public television / private television / soap opera / TV series / documentary / news

Teacher → Pupil Questions

- How do you rate the quality of TV stations in your country?
- Which channel offers the best news coverage, in your opinion?
- Do you ever stream television programs online? Which streaming services do you use?
- Would you ever download a TV program from the Internet? Do you worry about the legality of doing this?

Speaking activity

Compare two TV stations you watch by writing down a few strengths and weaknesses of each.

Exchange your list of strengths and weaknesses with a partner. Ask them about their list. Tell *them* about *yours*.

Report your partner's responses to the class.

Partner Interview

- What annoys you most about television?
- What are the differences between private and public television? Which do you prefer?
- If you could change one thing about the television stations in your country, what would it be?
- How many hours of television per day are too many, in your opinion?
- How much television would you allow/do you allow your children to watch?

Consolidation

Television has lost popularity with the younger generation, who are increasingly watching online.

Discuss briefly with a partner: Have your television-watching habits changed since online video has taken off? What do you think is the future for TV? Report your ideas to the class.

Time

Warm-up

What attitude do people have to time in your country? Is the attitude strict or flexible? How do you manage your time? Do you make lists? Give yourself deadlines? Describe your daily routine in terms of time.

Key Vocabulary

strict / flexible / time management / punctual / unpunctual / to meet a deadline / to miss a deadline / to be productive / productivity / to procrastinate

Teacher → Pupil Questions

- Which activities make you feel that time is passing quickly/slowly?
- Does commuting feel like a waste of time to you? How do you occupy yourself when you are waiting for a bus/train, et cetera?
- What would you do if you had more time?
- Are you a very punctual person? Does it annoy you when people are unpunctual?
- Do deadlines help you to be productive? Do you usually meet deadlines or miss deadlines?

Speaking activity

Ask a partner: Do you know anyone who tends to procrastinate instead of doing tasks? What is the best way to stop procrastinating? Do you have any strategies?

Share your strategies with a partner.

Partner Interview

- In the modern workplace, people find they need to do more tasks in less time. Do you have any strategies for staying productive under time pressure?
- Do you find meetings a waste of time? In your opinion, what makes a productive meeting? What makes an unproductive meeting?
- Do you have daylight saving time in your country? Do you think this is a good idea?
- If you could change one thing about the way your time is organised, what would it be?

Consolidation

Ask a partner: If you could go back in time to any historical period, which would you choose and why? What would be the advantages of living in that time period? What would be the disadvantages?

Report your partner's responses to the class.

Traditions & Customs

Warm-up

What is your favourite tradition? What traditions do you follow? Have you ever noticed any interesting customs while you were abroad?

Key Vocabulary

custom / tradition / to celebrate / to adapt / relevant / irrelevant / abroad / festival

Teacher → Pupil Questions

- Are there any traditions from other countries you would like to have in your culture?
- Is it traditional to eat particular food on special occasions in your country? Give a few examples (e.g. New year / Christian festivals / Islamic festivals).
- Which customs or traditions did you follow as a child that you don't follow anymore?
- Do you try to adapt to a country's customs when you visit that country? Why is that important?

Speaking activity

You work for a company that provides cross-cultural training for foreigners who want to do business in your country. You and a colleague (classmate) have been asked to write 5 Top Tips for Doing Business in [Your Country] for the company newsletter, including customs, body language and attitudes.

Share your tips with the class.

Partner Interview

- Which traditions do your parents follow that you don't?
- Describe an interesting tradition or custom from another country that you have heard about.
- What is the strangest custom your have heard of? What customs are there in *your* country that a visitor might find surprising?
- What traditions are practiced at weddings in your culture?

Consolidation

Which traditions are becoming more relevant? Which traditions are dying out?

With a partner, make a list of which traditions you think will *increase* in popularity in future another list of which traditions you think will *decrease* in popularity.

Discuss *why* you think this will happen and present your thoughts to the class.

Transport

Warm-up

What kind of transportation do you use for (a) short distances in your own city or town, (b) longer distances within your country, (c) travelling abroad? What is your favourite form of transport? What is your least favourite?

Key Vocabulary

to travel by car / to go on foot / to ride a bike / to drive a car / to get a taxi / to catch a bus / to commute / convenient / inconvenient / carbon footprint / annoying / independent

Teacher → Pupil Questions

- Which form of transportation do you think is the safest? Which is the most dangerous?
- If you could change one thing about the public transport system in your country, what would it be?
- What are the advantages and disadvantages of driving a car?
- What are the pros and cons of using the public transport system?

Speaking activity

Discuss briefly with a partner: What do you think transportation will be like 100 years in the future? What changes will there be in the next 100 years?

Present your ideas to the class.

Partner Interview

- How do you think transportation will change when oil finally runs out?
- Has concern for the environment ever stopped you taking the most convenient form of transport?
- How would you rate your carbon footprint?
- 'While air travel might be efficient, I find it incredibly annoying.' Do you agree or disagree?

Consolidation

What annoys you most about public transport? Many people find taking public transport annoying for one reason or another, either because it is not 'luxurious' enough, or because they don't feel independent.

With a partner, come up with 5 ways you could improve public transport in your area that would make it more appealing.

Present your ideas to the class.

Travel

Warm-up

Where did you go on your last holiday? Where are you planning on going for your next holiday? Which countries are top of the list of countries you would like to visit? Which countries don't appeal to you?

Key Vocabulary

a means of transport / route / school exchange / to be well travelled / to appeal to you / travel destination / travel companion / to take precautions

Teacher → Pupil Questions

- Have you been abroad many times? Where have you been?
- Do you consider yourself 'well travelled?'
- Which travel destinations did you most enjoy as a child? Have your tastes changed?
- Did you ever go on a school exchange when you were a teenager? Where did you go? How did you find the experience?
- Who is you favourite travel companion? Why?

Speaking activity

You have just won a round the world trip. Take a minute to decide (a) which route you will take, (b) which places you definitely want to see and (c) how you will travel (cruise ship, private jet, et cetera).

Describe your route to a partner and explain why you chose to see those particular places and why you chose that means of transport.

Partner Interview

- Which continents appeal to you most? Which don't appeal to you so much? Why/why not?
- Describe your best experience abroad. Describe your worst experience.
- Do you prefer to travel alone, with one other person, in a small group or in a large group? What are the advantages and disadvantages?
- Have you ever travelled anywhere dangerous? What precautions did you take?
- What precautions is it necessary to take, even when travelling in safer countries?

Consolidation

Ask a partner to compare their last two trips abroad. What were the positives and negatives of each trip?

Report your partner's responses to the class.

Vegetarian and Vegan

Warm-up

Are you a vegetarian, or have you ever considered becoming a vegetarian? Do you know many vegetarians? Did they become vegetarians for moral reasons, religious reasons, environmental reasons, or for health reasons?

Key Vocabulary

sustainable / to slaughter / ethical (reasons) / moral (reasons) / to try something out / to consider / acceptable / unacceptable / to produce (food) / well treated / badly treated

Teacher → Pupil Questions

- Have you ever tried vegetarianism for a few weeks? How did you find the experience?
- If you are a meat eater, do you enjoy vegetarian food?
- Have you ever been to a vegetarian restaurant? Describe the experience.
- What is the general attitude towards vegetarianism in your country? Does your country have a strong tradition of eating meat?
- Is vegetarian/vegan food in fashion in your country at the moment?

Speaking activity

How would the world be different if everyone was a vegetarian? With a partner, write a short list of things that would change if the world became vegetarian.

Then decide which points on your list are positive changes and which are negative changes.

Share your ideas with the class.

Partner Interview

- Do you think a vegetarian diet is healthier? Why/why not?
- Which mealtime would you miss the most if you became a vegetarian?
- Would you still eat meat if you had to kill all the animals yourself?
- Rearing animals for slaughter uses many times more water, land, oil and grain than growing vegetables. Is eating meat sustainable, in your opinion?

Consolidation

You and a partner would like to invite a vegetarian friend of yours to dinner. With a partner, decide what you will cook. Include a starter, main course and dessert.

Describe your meal to the class.

Weddings

Warm-up

Have you been to a lot of weddings? What customs/traditions do people practice at weddings in your country? What makes an enjoyable wedding in your opinion?

Key Vocabulary

marriage / customs / memorable / security / divorce / bride / groom / ceremony / guests / to celebrate / best man / bridesmaid / speech

Teacher → Pupil Questions

- Describe the most memorable wedding you have ever been to.
- Do you prefer small weddings or large weddings with hundreds of guests?
- What is the best age to get married, in your opinion?
- A large number of people meet their partners at weddings. Why do you think this is?

Speaking activity

Ask a partner to describe their dream wedding. If they are married, they should describe their *actual* wedding. Ask about the location, size, highlights, food, clothes, speeches and activities.

Partner Interview

- 'Men don't care about the wedding itself. It's more important for women to have a beautiful dress and be the centre of attention.' Do you agree or disagree?
- How do you feel when you go to a wedding and the couple get divorced a year or two later?
- 'Lots of people get married because they think it gives them security. In reality one in three marriages end in divorce, so being married doesn't actually make you more secure!' What do you think of this opinion?
- In developed countries, people are getting married later and later. Why do you think this is?

Consolidation

What advice would you give a young couple intending to get married?

Circulate and tell your advice to your classmates.

Afterwards, report to the class who you think gave the best advice and why.

Work-Life Balance

Warm-up

Do you work to live or live to work? Do you find your job stressful? How does your job compare with 10 years ago? Is it more stressful or less stressful?

Key Vocabulary

to be susceptible to something / burnout / recreation / to address an issue / suggestions / recommendations

Teacher → Pupil Questions

- What do you do to make sure you have a good work-life balance?
- Do you have a good way of dealing with stress?
- Have you ever been burnt out, or know anyone has become burnt out?
- Is admitting you are burnt out a taboo in your company (or country)?

Speaking activity

Some large companies have many recreation activities at the workplace for employees, including a gym, cafes and gaming rooms. Do you think having leisure activities in the workplace is a good idea?

With a partner, discuss the pros and cons of this idea.

Share your opinions with the class.

Partner Interview

- Are some personality types more susceptible to burnout?
- 'Modern employees are constantly under pressure to do more work in less time.' Do you agree?
- Does your company try to make sure employees have a good work-life balance?
- How would you like your company to address this issue?
- How important are: a) exercise, b) diet and c) family-life to a good work-life balance?

Consolidation

Your HR manager has asked you and your team to come up with a list of recommendations for reducing burnout and promoting a good work-life balance your company. What would you change in your company to achieve this?

Come up with at least 5 suggestions and present them to the class. Give reasons for your suggestions.

Youth and Aging

Warm-up

Which age have you found it most enjoyable to be so far in your life? What do you think is the best age to be? Why? What is the ideal age to live to?

Key Vocabulary

generation / to take care of / longevity / attitude / population / juvenile / childhood

Teacher → Pupil Questions

- Has the world changed for the better or for the worse since you were a child?
- Are the youth of today different from when you were in your youth? How?
- What do you think the older generation can teach the younger generation?
- What can the younger generation teach the older generation?
- Does the state take care of older people in your country? How?

Speaking activity

Which of the following quotes do you like most and why? Which comes closest to your own attitude?

- 'Youth is wasted on the young.' (Oscar Wilde)
- 'Age is a question of mind over matter. If you don't mind, it doesn't matter.' (Leroy Paige)
- 'Time may be a great healer, but it's a lousy beautician.' (Anon)

Report to the class.

Partner Interview

- What do you think is the secret to longevity (a long life)?
- Does your country have an aging population or a young population? What are the pros and cons?
- Do you think that older people make better leaders?
- If you were part of a team working on a company project, would you prefer to work with (a) mostly older team members, (b) mostly younger team members or (c) a mixture?
- 'Youth is a state of mind.' Do you agree or disagree?

Consolidation

You are flying a small passenger jet with your co-pilot when it develops engine trouble. On board are 3 passengers: an 80-year-old Nobel Prize winner (who still publishes the occasional paper), a 40-year-old high school English teacher and a juvenile young offender serving 6 months for dealing soft drugs. You have 1 parachute, which will save the life of 1 passenger. Talk to your co-pilot and decide who will get the parachute. Report your reasons to the class.

Printed in Germany
by Amazon Distribution
GmbH, Leipzig